To Renew America

Newt Gingrich

To Renew America

HarperCollins*Publishers*

HarperCollins books may be purchased for educational, business, or sales promotional use. For information please write: Special Markets Department, HarperCollins Publishers, Inc., 10 East 53rd Street, New York, NY 10022.

Library of Congress Cataloging-in-Publication Data

Gingrich, Newt.
    To renew America / Newt Gingrich.
      p. cm.
    Includes index.
    ISBN 0-06-017336-X
    1. United States—Politics and government—20th century.   2. United States—Social policy.   3. United States—Economic policy.   4. United States—Moral conditions.   5. Information society—United States.   I. Title.
JK424.G56   1995
973.929—dc20   95-11183

---

95 96 97 98 99 ❖/RRD 10 9 8 7 6 5

To Marianne, who made it all worthwhile

Contents

Acknowledgments

This book was a team effort in several respects. The basic concepts expressed here have been developed over a number of years and bear the imprint of many friends, coworkers, students, and colleagues. Most notably, I am indebted to Jack Kemp, Ronald Reagan, Ken Duberstein, and Vin Weber; also my current colleagues in the House of Representatives (especially Bob Walker, Dick Armey, and John Kasich, but including in one way or another virtually every Republican member) and the staff members who helped shape the Contract with America in both strategy and execution. Of them, I especially wish to thank Dan Meyer, Jack Howard, Len Swinehart, Karen Feaga, Ed Kutler, Arne Christenson, Rachel Phillips, Tony Blankley, Allan Lipsett, Amy Clark, Barry Hutchison, Hardy Lott, and Anne Beighey.

Actually, the development of these ideas goes even farther back, to Pete Jensen at Georgia Tech, Jerry Pournelle, Jim Baen, Bill Bennett, and especially to a number of friends who have traded ideas with me over the decades: Owen Roberts, Joe Gaylord, Steve Hanser, Nancy Desmond, Jane Fortson, Jeff Eisenach, Grover Norquist, Heather Higgins, John Fund, Bill Kristol, Barbara Lawton, Bill Loughrey, Terry Maple, and Kathleen Minnix. Special thanks also to Tim Mescon, Betty Siegel, and Floyd Falany who made my earlier courses possible.

For their support of my intellectual and personal development, I thank many relatives and friends, especially my mom and dad, Kit and Bob Gingrich, my sister Rob, my brother, Randy, my aunt Loma and uncle Cal, my aunt Louise and uncle Bruce, my grandmother Daugherty. Thanks also to dear friends Paul Walker and Jim Tilton, whose love, patience, and wisdom shaped my understanding of life and of America.

I count myself especially lucky in my two daughters and their husbands, who enrich our lives and deepen our understanding in a hundred ways: Kathy and Paul Lubbers and Jackie and Mark Zyla.

Finally, the book would never have come about had it not been for the collaborative efforts of Lynn Chu, my literary agent, Jan Baran, for solving the complex legal and editorial requirements of a book-writing Speaker of the House, Adrian Zackheim, my editor, and Bill Tucker, my cowriter, who truly performed a miracle under the most difficult circumstances. I thank the entire staff at HarperCollins, my publisher, for their extraordinary professionalism. And finally, for the hundreds of hours of brainstorming, critiquing, editing, arguing, supporting, and cheerleading, I thank the main collaborator of my life, my wife, Marianne.

PART ONE

Visions and Strategies

CHAPTER 1

The Six Challenges
Facing America

These are the best of times and the worst of times, as Charles Dickens wrote. On the one hand, America is the leading country on the planet, with the largest economy and providing the opportunity to pursue happiness to more different kinds of people from more backgrounds than any society in history. On the other hand, our civilization is decaying, with an underclass of poverty and violence growing in our midst and an economy hard pressed to compete with those of Germany, Japan, and China.

We can look around us with both great satisfaction and great concern. We are the people who led the coalition that defeated Nazi Germany, Imperial Japan, and fascist Italy and then led a worldwide coalition that contained the Soviet Empire for a half century before its collapse. While we as a people were winning our battles around the world, here at home our elites were deserting us. For the past thirty years, we have been influenced to abandon our culture and seem to have lost faith in the core values, traditions, and institutions of our civilization. The intellectual nonsense propagated since 1965—in the media, on university campuses, even among our religious and political leaders—now threatens to cripple our ability to teach the next generation to be Americans. We have placed men on the moon, led the world in molecular medicine, and entered the age of computers and telecommunications. Yet we have simultaneously allowed our schools to decay to the point that our children regularly score below all others of the industrialized world in math and science. We risk not being able to understand the very world we have invented.

It is impossible to know which of these tendencies—our great strengths or our great weaknesses—will prevail. Will historians record America as a meteor that emerged as a world power in the twentieth century, then found itself unable to solve its own internal problems and rapidly declined into a regional power? Or will they remember America as the center of freedom that, having defeated its foreign enemies, found the moral and political courage to revitalize its civilization and lead the human race to even greater levels of freedom, prosperity, and security? It is impossible to know today which story will be told to our descendants.

It is clear, however, that the answer matters both to ourselves and to our neighbors on this globe. If we fail to reform, the consequences will be incalculable. The underclass of poverty and violence will continue to grow. Our economy will gradually fall farther and farther behind those of our best competitors. Our vision will blur and our civilization continue to lose its focus as fewer and fewer people learn about our culture, traditions, and institutions. We will have fewer scientific and technological breakthroughs. Our quality of health and life will diminish. In this weakened state, we will be unable to sustain our military and diplomatic responsibilities and the world will break into isolated and competing blocs characterized by internal and external violence. Rwanda, Bosnia, Chechnya, and Somalia will all be harbingers of the future.

If we can reform ourselves, on the other hand, there is every reason to believe our best days are still ahead. A renewed and reinvigorated America that educates all its children could compete with any country. An America that has replaced the culture of poverty and violence with a culture of opportunity would be the safest, most prosperous place on the globe. An entrepreneurial America that embraces science and innovation would progress at a fantastic pace, opening a vastly greater range of choices to its people than any civilization in history. Such a revitalized America could sustain its military and diplomatic responsibilities with ease and still find the world eager to be led toward greater prosperity, security, and freedom. Once again, America would be the last, best hope on earth.

The choice between these two futures is stark and decisive. Either we will pull ourselves together for the effort or we will continue to decay. There is virtually no middle ground. An America that arouses itself to replace the culture of poverty and violence and insists that its children learn the core values of American civilization is an America that will find each challenge more invigorating than the last. But an America that remains passive and apathetic, divided and confused, will be on the road to decline.

I believe the task can be accomplished. I believe we can revitalize American society, restore the greatness of American civilization, and reinvigorate the American economy while we remake the structure of American government. My optimism is based on the simple belief that we have seen enough of the decay and failure of the welfare state to be ready to restore our historic principles. Older Americans who grew up with the certainty and convictions of World War II and the Cold War are eager for a rebirth of American values. Baby boomers who grew up with the counterculture are now sober and mature enough to see that many of its principles simply don't work. Younger Americans—from Generation X on down—know from personal experience that a culture of violence, ignorance, and government debt poses a severe threat to their future. When more people below the age of thirty believe in UFOs than believe that their Social Security pensions will be waiting for them when they retire, you know we are ready for a change in course.

America has had many similar reform eras. Almost once a generation, we have reached the point where the political system is so out of touch with the new needs and new realities that we require a momentous transformation to set us free once again. The Revolutionary War, the Federalist period, Jeffersonian democracy, the Jacksonian era, Lincoln and the antislavery crusade, the Progressive Era, FDR and the New Deal, the civil rights movement—each represented a tremendous burst of energy and upheaval, conflict and rebirth.

Now we are entering a similar era—one that saw its beginnings in the Goldwater campaign, saw some success during the Reagan years, and has finally come to full flower during the historic congressional elections of 1994. As during every reform era, there are sincere people who favor the changes, just as there are equally sincere people who will do everything they can to prop up the old order. It may be more than a decade before the forces that have been set in motion achieve their full result. But most students of American history would agree that another era of American reform has begun.

America is a great country with good people living in it. For this reason alone, I am optimistic that the necessary reforms will be embraced and our civilization renewed. However, as my grandmother taught me, God helps those who help themselves. In the past, when America has gotten in trouble, we have always been fortunate to find a generation of leaders who were prepared to rise to the challenge and step outside the normal political currents to engage the overriding issues of the day. This book represents an effort to define those issues.

Let me begin by outlining the six major changes that I

believe are necessary to leave our children with an America that is prosperous, free, and safe:

1. We must reassert and renew American civilization. From the arrival of English-speaking colonists in 1607 until 1965, there was one continuous civilization built around a set of commonly accepted legal and cultural principles. From the Jamestown colony and the Pilgrims, through de Tocqueville's *Democracy in America,* up to the Norman Rockwell paintings of the 1940s and 1950s, there was a clear sense of what it meant to be an American. Our civilization is based on a spiritual and moral dimension. It emphasizes personal responsibility as much as individual rights. Since 1965, however, there has been a calculated effort by cultural elites to discredit this civilization and replace it with a culture of irresponsibility that is incompatible with American freedoms as we have known them. Our first task is to return to teaching Americans about America and teaching immigrants how to become Americans. Until we reestablish a legitimate moral-cultural standard, our civilization is at risk.

2. We must accelerate America's entry into the Third Wave Information Age. The scientific and technological changes going on around us are far more significant and unprecedented than we have recognized. The opportunities to improve our lives are almost unimaginable. Scientists, engineers, and entrepreneurs are creating a future of enormous power and potential. Yet we are often remarkably incapable of understanding these changes or fitting them into our everyday lives. If we can grasp the true significance of these changes, we can lead the world into the Information Age and leave our children a country unmatched in wealth, power, and opportunity. If we fail, we will at best have a lower standard of living and at worst

find that another country has moved into the new era so decisively that it can dominate us. Second only to renewing our civilization is making the intellectual investment necessary to understand these changes and harness them to our lasting advantage.

3. We must rethink our competition in the world market. The world is rapidly becoming a place of serious and intense economic competition. The best of our competitors are very, very good. Yet we can only lead the world to freedom if we remain the predominant economy. When the dollar falls against the yen and the mark, America's prestige and ability to lead fall with it. Eventually, our children's standards of living will fall as well. We must rethink all the things that inhibit our ability to compete: regulation, litigation, taxation, education, welfare, the structure of our government bureaucracies. We want our labor to add the highest value so that we can be the most productive and effective competitor on earth. Only then will our children be assured good jobs and higher take-home pay. Given the quality of our competition, this is going to mean real work and real change.

4. We must replace the welfare state with an opportunity society. Every American is entitled to a life filled with opportunity. After all, we are endowed by our Creator with certain inalienable rights, among which are life, liberty, and the pursuit of happiness. Yet today too many Americans are bound in bureaucracies and antihuman regulations by which families are destroyed, the work ethic is undermined, male responsibility is made irrelevant, and young mothers find themselves trapped in a world where "income maintenance" replaces opportunity. No civilization can survive for long with twelve-year-olds having babies, fifteen-year-olds killing one another, seventeen-year-olds dying of AIDS, and eighteen-year-olds getting diplomas they can't read. Yet every night on the local

news, you and I watch the welfare state undermining our society. The vast majority of Americans (96 percent by one recent poll) is ready to admit that the welfare state has failed. They have lost faith that government can improve the lot of the poor and want their children reeducated in core American values. We simply must abandon the welfare state and move to an opportunity society.

5. America is too big, too diverse, and too free to be run by bureaucrats sitting in office buildings in one city. We must replace our centralized, micromanaged, Washington-based bureaucracy with a dramatically decentralized system more appropriate to a continent-wide country. As I listen to stories from around our nation about particularly foolish, arrogant, and uninformed behavior from Washington, I am struck by the conceit that led people to believe a country this size could be managed by people who never even visited your town. How can your affairs be handled by people who don't have a clue as to how much things have changed since the last time a government inspector came through? We simply must shift power and responsibility back to state governments, local governments, nonprofit institutions, and—most important of all—individual citizens. "Closer is better" should be the rule of thumb for our decision making; less power in Washington and more back home, our consistent theme.

6. We must be honest about the cost of government programs and balance the federal budget. Medicare will be in serious financial trouble by 1996 and will start going bankrupt by 2002. If the federal budget remains in deficit, the Treasury will not be able to repay the notes in the Social Security Trust Fund and the baby boomers will see their retirement pensions evaporate. At the current rates of borrowing, a child born in 1995 will pay $187,000—an estimated $3,500 per year over the course of his or her working lifetime—just to pay off the *interest* on his or her

share of the debt, without beginning to reduce principle and relieve the burden on the next generation. If you are a senior citizen, you need fiscal honesty so we can save Medicare. If you are a baby boomer, you need fiscal honesty so you can have Social Security when you retire. If you are a young person, you will need fiscal honesty in order to have economic opportunity in your lifetime. The American tradition used to be to pay off the mortgage and leave the kids the farm. Now we are selling off the farm and leaving the kids the mortgage. No civilization can survive if parents and grandparents cheat their children by leaving them crushed with debt. We have a moral obligation to balance the budget now.

In 1936, President Franklin Delano Roosevelt told the American public, "Our generation has a rendezvous with destiny." That generation courageously met its challenge—and triumphed. Now it is our turn. If we rise to the task, if we meet the challenges of our era, we will leave our children with a much safer and more prosperous nation. If we fail, our children will inherit all the problems we have failed to resolve—plus much more. We will have squandered their inheritance and undermined their freedom.

I have spent much of my life studying and working on the problems of how civilizations survive. It began when I was surprisingly young. In the next chapter, I am going to carry you back through some of the personal experiences that led me to believe a nation must continually attend to the challenges that confront it. From there, I shall outline in more detail the six major changes I believe we are facing.

Later I shall review the development of the Contract with America and the drama of its implementation during the 1994 campaign and the first one hundred days of Congress. I shall also address what I see as the critical issues that we as a nation must confront even as we overcome the six vital challenges of renewing our civilization—issues that will engage the energies of every American until the millennium's end.

Finally, I shall explore the romantic idealism that led our Founding Fathers to pledge their lives, their fortunes, and their sacred honor to their country and suggest a twenty-first-century vision worthy of that same kind of commitment.

The issues are clear before us. The choice is ours. Let us begin.

CHAPTER 2

Beginnings

In 1957 my dad was sent to Orléans, France, to serve in the Communications Zone of the American forces in Europe ("Com Z," as we called it). The city—once rescued for the French by Joan of Arc—was still being rebuilt after World War II bomb damage. Because my dad was a junior officer, we could not get housing with the American military. Instead, for about three months, we lived in a downtown Orléans hotel. There we were, my mom, my dad, my two younger sisters, and myself, living in one small room. (My sister Candy was not born until 1966.) We had a two-burner Coleman stove on which my mom cooked and a bathtub down the hall that was shared with several other residents on the floor. You had to schedule use of the bathroom to take a bath and paid extra for using it. In our own room there was a bidet—something a thirteen-year-old American boy had obviously never seen—a toilet and a washbasin.

After a few months of this spartan life, my dad found a beautiful château in Beaugency sur Loire, about twenty miles from Orléans. There we had three stories with a huge kitchen, dining and living rooms on the ground floor, and several enclosed acres with a terrace leading down to the river. A gardener kept the grounds while his wife served as maid and cook for the owners, a Parisian family who came down occasionally on vacation. For a young American, this was extravagant living—made possible by a strong dollar and an invincible American economy. Winning the war certainly made life easier for the victors.

Living in Beaugency meant a long ride in an army bus to Orléans American High School, but it also meant playing among young French kids and learning a lot about a country that was clearly in trouble.

France in 1957 was in the midst of an identity crisis. Its government was called the Fourth Republic, and it was generally regarded as weak and incompetent. Immediately after the war, General Charles de Gaulle, the hero of the French Liberation, had become so disgusted with his nation's weakness that he resigned the presidency in 1946 and retired to his home at Colombey-les-deux-Églises to write his memoirs. On occasion, he gave speeches encouraging the Gaullist movement, which called for a nationalist, high-technology France with a stronger, more accountable government.

France had been defeated by the Nazis in 1940, only weeks after the German offensive began. While northern France was occupied by the Germans, southern France had remained nominally independent under the Vichy regime (based in the town of Vichy). Freedom returned only when the Liberation began at Normandy on June 6, 1944. Much of the French transportation system had been destroyed during preparation for the invasion and the fighting that followed.

After World War II, France had engaged in a long and bitter war in Vietnam, which drained both men and money. Then a horrified, war-weary population found itself engaged in a bitter civil war over Algeria. Faced with these continuing burdens on its economy, the French were unable to maintain a sound currency. During the year and a half we lived in France, the annual inflation rate was more than 100 percent and still rising. We Americans were paid in a funny money called "scrip." Our dollars were so powerful that, had they been introduced into the French economy, they would have destroyed the franc overnight.

As a young American, I found myself fascinated by the impact these complications of international finance had on us. Our scrip—which resembled Monopoly money—was designed to keep us buying things at the post commissary, instead of competing unfairly with the French people. This, of course, led us to buy things in our American stores and barter them into the French economy. Western string ties were particularly popular among the gypsies who ran the traveling fairs that came through town regularly. I remember we would go to the post exchange and buy all the string ties in stock, then go to a fair and start swapping our genuine American western wear for cheap (but to us exotic and wonderful) French champagne. This early experience made me think quite a lot about the concept of money as a medium of exchange. The inflation rate taught me that the value of money is by no means certain and that a decaying government with a weak currency can quickly undermine people's faith in its political leadership. When a government cheats its own people by inflating the currency rather than facing tough political decisions, it is inviting trouble.

In the summer of 1958, my dad was transferred from Orléans to Stuttgart, Germany. Shortly after, the French Fourth Republic fell and de Gaulle was recalled to public life. French army paratroopers were planning literally to invade Paris from Algeria and overthrow the Fourth Republic. De Gaulle intervened and created the Fifth Republic. In a series of brilliant maneuvers, he ended the war in Algeria, modernized the French military, stabilized the French franc, encouraged French economic growth, and reestablished France's stability and self-esteem—all while surviving a number of sophisticated attempts on his life. The framework he created still serves as the core of the French nation today. I watched this bold renewal of French life, first as a high school student in Stuttgart and then as a college student at Emory University in Atlanta.

This personal exposure to a nation in agony left an indelible impression on me. I recognized that nations can undermine themselves through inadequate policies and moral collapse. Weak leadership and a refusal to confront problems rapidly lead to national decay. Successful leaders must be prepared to gamble everything—as de Gaulle did many times during his career.

While we lived in France I had one other experience that changed my life. At Easter in 1958 we visited the battlefield of Verdun. Our host was a friend of my father's, an army officer who had been drafted in World War II and served in the Philippines. He had been captured by the Japanese, forced on one of the death marches, and spent three and a half years in a Japanese prison camp, suffering permanent damage to his health as the result. I still have a photograph from that weekend.

For two days, my parents and I toured the site of one of the largest battles on the Western Front during World War I. Over an eight-month period in 1916, more than 700,000 men were killed or wounded on that battlefield. The attack was part of a plan by the Germans to draw the French army into a battle of attrition. Before it was over, both sides had poured almost inconceivable numbers of men and resources into the struggle. In the end, both the French and the Germans were drained and exhausted.

The resources a country will expend when it thinks its survival is at stake are simply enormous. We walked through one fortress built right into a mountain where the French had poured enough concrete to rebuild Orléans. The purpose was to bring artillery shells in the back side on a tiny railroad through the mountain so they could be fired out the other side at the advancing Germans. I was amazed at the scale of investment needed to survive an effort at conquest by a neighboring country.

The human cost of war was driven home to me even more

vividly by a visit to the Ossuary. This is a large building whose glassed-in basement contains the bones of approximately 100,000 men whose bodies were blown apart or left rotting in the fields during the long battle. It is an extraordinary monument to man's potential for inhumanity.

But the most shocking thing to me about Verdun was in a way the most ordinary. On our last day, we drove downtown past houses that still had holes in their roofs from being hit by artillery shells. We had seen the same kind of damage many times around Orléans. Trying to impress our host, I commented how similar this unrepaired World War II damage was to what we were used to seeing near the base. Imagine my shock when he told me that this was artillery damage from *World War I*!

How shocking that a city could still be wounded forty-two years later—that it had not yet marshaled the resources, energy, or organization to recover! For some reason, the notion that an artillery shell striking a private home could leave it damaged for three times longer than my lifetime (I was fourteen at the time) was so staggering that it has never left my mind. To this day, when I see the tragedy in Sarajevo or the fighting in Chechnya, I am reminded of the terrible ability of humans to cause pain to one another and of the terrible risks a country and its people run when they underestimate the effort it takes to remain safe and free.

Until we visited Verdun, I believed I was going to be a zoo director or a vertebrate paleontologist specializing in dinosaurs or early mammals of the Paleocene and Eocene. My interest in politics was focused largely on how to get a zoo for my hometown of Harrisburg, Pennsylvania. After that weekend, my ambitions changed.

That summer, when my dad's transfer to Stuttgart came through, we packed our belongings in our station wagon and the five of us plus our dog, Pride, drove across France and Germany. The morning we arrived in Stuttgart, American forces moved into Lebanon to prop up the established government, which was in a civil war. The crisis was part of a larger Middle Eastern outbreak that included a coup in Iraq and an attempted coup in Jordan. The situation was so tense that as soon as my dad saw the *Stars and Stripes* newspaper at breakfast he reported in and we were left alone for three days. My mom took care of us while we awaited the outcome.

Stuttgart was the main headquarters of the Seventh U.S. Army, and the looming threat of war was vastly more real and intense than it had ever been in France. Alerts were called on a regular basis to test whether the army could move into the field faster than the Soviets could bomb our headquarters. I remember vividly hearing the phone ring at four in the morning and listening to my dad get up and leave on an alert. I could look out my bedroom window and see the army moving into the field in its combat gear. As I watched the long parade move in an orderly and impressive manner, it gradually occurred to me that the folks being left behind who would be casualties if the Soviets did bomb were my mother, my sisters, and myself. My mother kept a footlocker of survival gear and an evacuation map to help lead us to Switzerland in the event of a real crisis. Now that the Cold War is over, these precautions may seem exaggerated, but to a generation raised on Pearl Harbor, the Bataan death march, and the surprise attack and bloody war in Korea, they made eminent sense.

In August 1958, I had a summer job as gardener for our housing complex. It gave me time to think about Verdun and all I had learned in the past five months. To this day, I can remember putting in the sod one warm sunny August afternoon and suddenly reaching the conclusion that civilizations can die. I realized that our civilization was facing a mortal threat from the Soviet empire and that some people had to be willing to dedicate their lives to protecting our way of life, our freedom, and our people. I also concluded that this was the kind of challenge that could not be passed off to others. If it were truly a moral question of whether we as a free people would survive, then I had an obligation to do my share of the job.

I don't know how many of my thoughts that summer were born of an adolescent search for identity and how many came from my grandmother Daugherty's deeply intense Lutheran teachings, from my admiration of my father's sense of duty, honor, and country, or from my need for a mission to give meaning to my life. Perhaps it was simply that someone had to put helping one's country and trying to understand what is needed to survive at the center of his or her life. In any event, that summer I decided, in the innocently solemn way young people sometimes have, that I would dedicate my life to understanding what it takes for a free people to survive and to helping my country and the cause of freedom.

Whatever the underlying motivations, the results were very real. I immediately began studying history and reading books about politics. In my sophomore English class my teacher allowed me to write a paper on the balance of world power. Having your father stationed at Seventh Army headquarters is great for going to the command librarian and asking what books you ought to read to learn about military power. That high school experience was the beginning of an in-depth grounding in military history and military analysis that has served me well ever since.

In January 1960, we received orders for Fort Benning, Georgia. We sailed on a military transport ship from Bremerhaven to New York City. Crossing the Atlantic for eight days in midwinter as the only adolescent boy on board gave me the time to walk the ship and reconsider the whole question of spending my life on such a burdensome historic quest. After a year and a half of studying, it was obvious that politics and government are a difficult path and that it would take a tremendously focused life to be effective in trying to meet the challenges of the future. My conclusion was that there was no moral choice except to immerse myself in the process of learning how to lead and how to be effective.

After a month of visiting relatives in Harrisburg, we moved to Fort Benning, where my introduction to practical politics began. As a junior in high school, my best friend, Jim Tilton, and I traipsed across Columbus, Georgia, to join the Republican Party. Jim was the student body president, a varsity athlete in three sports, and a National Merit scholarship finalist. (Tragically, Jim died several years ago of pancreatic cancer. We had been best friends for thirty years, and he had been one of the most wonderful and most stable parts of my life.) That day, however, we were just teenage boys on a foolish errand. After walking for nearly two hours in the warm spring afternoon, we found no one home at the county chairman's house. It was a tribute to our determination, if not to our common sense, that we returned a few weeks later and successfully volunteered.

The 1960 Nixon-Lodge campaign was my first serious exposure to phone banks, party headquarters, stuffing envelopes, and the long hours of sheer drudgery that are at the heart of a political campaign. The Georgia of that era was a deeply conservative and Democratic state that gave John F. Kennedy his biggest margin of victory (bigger than in Rhode Island or Massachusetts). State politics were dominated by a one-party machine, which was in turn dominated by the "county unit system," which guaranteed that the rural counties would choose the governor. Each county was given a number of voting "units" in the Democratic primary, with the biggest county getting only three times the number of the smallest county. As a result, a vote in Echols County (the smallest) was worth over nine hundred votes in Fulton County, the largest. This gerrymandering meant—as Gene Talmadge used to boast—that you could win the nomination for governor or senator without carrying a county that had a streetcar. Since the legislature and congressional seats were similarly gerrymandered, a state whose economy and culture were rapidly modernizing around Atlanta retained a political system that was a throwback to the turn of the century.

This intense bias toward very small, very rural counties gave a tremendous advantage to rural machines dominated by sheriffs and county commissioners. Because these districts were poor, the pressure toward graft and corruption was almost overwhelming. The system of "courthouse machines" ultimately led to one of the most colorful and most corrupt governors in the country, Marvin Griffin. *Reader's Digest* once ran an article recounting his scandals and colorful stories. My favorite was his retort when reporters discovered he had bought boats without bottoms. "Those are for the state parks without lakes," he responded. Everyone laughed, but his patronage and graft controlled the state legislature.

Besides being overwhelmingly Democratic and corrupt (Griffin had been out of office only two years), the Georgia I entered was bitterly segregationist. It always amuses me when reporters and columnists assume I must be a traditional southern conservative with, they hint, racist and redneck roots. As an army brat, my first experience of legal segregation was shocking. In Columbus, schools, bathrooms, and water fountains were all segregated. I had always gone to school with children of all backgrounds in Pennsylvania, Kansas, France, and Germany, and had never thought much about it. People were people and you learned to live with everyone. In 1962 I found myself in my first political argument about race, listening to a yellow-dog Democrat from Cairo (deep in south Georgia) patiently explain how blacks were not fully human and that any effort to integrate was biologically doomed to fail.

Segregation had been erected by the southern Democratic Party to give power to white elites by splitting poor people of both races. Segregation was bitterly defended by southern white Democrats while being challenged by a coalition of northern Democrats and Republicans. I arrived in Georgia at the high-water mark of the coalition between Georgia blacks and the emerging middle class of Georgians and Yankee immigrants that Samuel Lubbell describes so well in his studies of American politics. For an Eisenhower Republican, the 1960 Nixon-Lodge ticket was a progressive reform ticket, while the forces of corruption, racism, and one-party rule were all in the Georgia Democratic Party.

Tom Murphy, speaker of the Georgia House and the longest serving speaker in the country, is in many respects the last vestige of the old wool-hat, county courthouse Democratic Party. His intelligence, toughness, and hard work have kept him the dominant figure in Georgia politics even though the forces of the world that created him have largely disappeared. It is also a tribute to Murphy's political doggedness that he has dedicated much of his energies over the last decade to trying to destroy my political career. He recruited and financed candidates against me and in 1991 set the abolition of my congressional district through reapportionment as his highest goal. He succeeded, but I survived narrowly in an entirely new district. While I disagree with his politics, I admire his tenacity and toughness. He taught me a number of lessons about power that helped me become leader of the House Republican Party and Speaker of the House.

Upon coming back from Europe, I also began immersing myself in history and the changes that threaten civilizations. I found myself reading both into the past and into the future. Arnold Toynbee's *A Study of History* is a ten-volume attempt to trace the history of the human race. Isaac Asimov's Foundation series is a three-volume introduction to civilizations as seen through a science fiction epic. Each in its own way has had a profound influence on my life.

As a young man, Toynbee had also been influenced by the Great War. The death of a generation of young British soldiers drew him into a lifetime of study about what shapes civilizations.

Toynbee's thesis was called "challenge and response." He argued that every civilization sooner or later encounters a challenge that threatens its very existence. At that point, the key question becomes how its leadership elites respond and whether they are adequate to the task. Toynbee ranged widely, noting that solving one generation's challenge did not necessarily mean the civilization would rise to the next one. It was quite possible for a civilization to be successful for a long time and then suddenly fall apart. The challenges also might change dramatically. One generation could face military challenges while the next would be challenged by religion, politics, economics, or technology.

Ranging across history, Toynbee proposed an antidote to the insular complacency of the time, which said that having beaten Nazi Germany and Imperial Japan, we were bound to be successful in the long run. In Toynbee's view, Han China had been the dominant economic and cultural system on the planet for nearly two thousand years until it failed to modernize in the nineteenth century and ended up collapsing in the face of Western European economic and technological progress. (To Toynbee, European military advantages were almost entirely a function of political, economic, and technological advantages.)

The short view of two hundred years of American history was rapidly put in perspective by an analysis that noted that the Roman domination of the Mediterranean world lasted about six hundred years. Even Rome's seeming endurance faded next to the additional thousand years of Byzantine survival. So broad was Toynbee's sweep that he could mention the three great Mesoamerican civilizations (Maya, Inca, and Aztec) and include them in an analysis with pharaonic Egypt, Mesopotamia, and the Indus Valley.

A Study of History liberated me from any sense that we inevitably know how to keep America strong. It also engendered in me a deep sense that every generation faces the potential of serious challenges and that failure to respond effectively could mean the end of your civilization in a remarkably short period of time. Consider the speed with which the Aztecs and Incas collapsed when an extraordinarily small European force was brought to bear against them. Whenever someone suggests that we can be complacent about survival in our age of rapid technological change, I wonder what they would have predicted for the Indo-American civilizations a few years before the Spanish reached the New World.

While Toynbee was impressing me with the history of civilizations, Isaac Asimov was shaping my view of the future in equally profound ways. As a very young man, Asimov wrote the Foundation trilogy. This three-volume work—*Foundation, Foundation and Empire*, and *Second Foundation*—remains one of the classics of science fiction.

Essentially, Asimov took the fall of Rome and turned it into a science fiction novel in which the Roman Empire became the Galactic Empire. The Catholic Church's role in maintaining civilized knowledge through the Dark and Middle Ages is played by a secular group of intellectuals called "The Foundation."

For a high school student who loved history, Asimov's most exhilarating invention was the "psychohistorian" named Hari Selden. The term does not refer to Freudian analysis but to a kind of probabilistic forecasting of the future of whole civilizations. The premise was that, while you cannot predict individual behavior, you can develop a pretty accurate sense of mass behavior. Pollsters and advertisers now make a good living off the same theory.

In Asimov's work, Hari Selden was capable of forecasting the decline of the entire Galactic empire. While the Foundation scholars were incapable of stopping the Empire's decline, they could compile knowledge and teach small cadres in a way that would limit the Dark Ages and accelerate the eventual Renaissance. Asimov did not believe in a mechanistic world. Instead, to Asimov, human beings always hold their fate in their own hands. Indeed, there are few novels that reflect better Toynbee's view of history than the Foundation trilogy.

These pivotal works focused my attention on the fate of civilizations. I came to realize that, while most people were immersed in day-to-day activities, daily behavior actually takes place within a much larger context of constantly changing global forces. The young French children I played with in Beaugency had lost fathers in World War II. My father's friend had had his life indelibly changed by three and a half years in a Japanese prisoner-of-war camp. Southern blacks could never have broken the back of legal segregation without the help of the federal government. Again and again, I realized, large-scale events create the framework within which ordinary people lead their lives.

The same is true today. We have created a civilization that is, by all odds, the greatest the planet has ever known. But we are now faced with a series of challenges, some of them routine on the scale of history, but others dangerous and unprecedented.

In proposing an American Renewal, I do so after having spent a long time thinking about the challenges we are facing and the responses we need. If the proposals I outline in this book seem ambitious, it is because I believe they reflect the magnitude of the challenges that face us. We are certainly not the first civilization to confront moral decay from within. But we are definitely *the first generation in American history* to face such a challenge.

This book will discuss the major challenges that confront us as a people today. They are, in fact—as Toynbee has illustrated—the kinds of challenges that all enduring civilizations must eventually meet and overcome if they are to survive. Unlike many other civilizations, however, we have an extraordinarily instructive text by which to guide ourselves—*our own history*. As I will show, becoming more aware of our own history and recovering parts of our lost heritage promises a solution to many of our problems.

Having earned our place as a great civilization, we should not be surprised to find ourselves facing challenges similar to those that other civilizations have faced before us. As Toynbee has shown, it is not the nature of these challenges, but the *quality of our response* to them that will determine our future.

With all this in mind, let us consider the challenges that lie before us.

PART TWO

The Six Challenges

CHAPTER 3

Reasserting and Renewing American Civilization

The central challenge to our generation is to reassert and renew American civilization. By definition, any civilization goes only a generation deep. If the next generation fails to learn what makes America tick, then our country could change decisively overnight.

This is not merely an academic abstraction. Look at how rapidly Nazi Germany and Imperial Japan changed from previous generations—and how quickly these malignant cultures were replaced by American models of the rule of law, free speech, and democracy once the war ended. Look at how rapidly Communism supplanted fascism in East Germany—and how rapidly West German rules and habits have replaced the Communist model since the Berlin Wall came tumbling down. Look at how quickly every country in the former Soviet empire has begun to assert new ways of doing things. While there are still residual influences of Lenin and Stalin, it is astonishing how rapidly their statues and their ideas have been replaced.

America is an idea, the most idea-based civilization in history. To be an American is to embrace a set of values and living habits that have flourished on this continent for nearly four hundred years. Virtually anyone can become American simply by learning the ideas and habits of being an American. When I talk with Henry Kissinger or Arnold Schwarzenegger, it is clear from their accents that they started somewhere else, but it is equally clear from their attitudes and behavior that they have become Americans.

Up until the mid–1960s children and immigrants alike were taught how to be American. From ceremonies (the Pledge of Allegiance, the opening prayer, "The Star-Spangled Banner") to historic holidays (the study of the Pilgrims at Thanksgiving, Washington and Lincoln on their birthdays) to stories in the schoolbooks, everyone absorbed a sense of how to be an American. Even myths such as Washington cutting down the cherry tree and not being able to tell a lie had a larger truth. Portrayed as the Father of Our Country, Washington was seen as the indispensable man, the individual on whose character and moral strength the nation was founded.

In the mid–1960s, this long-held consensus began to founder. The counterculture began to repudiate middle-class values—even though the creators of that counterculture were clearly middle class themselves. Multiculturalism switched the emphasis from proclaiming allegiance to the common culture to proclaiming the virtues (real or imagined) of a particular ethnicity, sect, or tribe. "Situational ethics" and "deconstructionism"—the belief that there are no general rules of behavior—began to supplant the centuries-old struggle to establish universal standards of right and wrong.

All this has led to a collapse in our ability to teach ethical behavior to our own people. Traditional history has been replaced by the notion that every group is entitled to its own version of the past. Moral standards have been replaced by "role-playing." Time once spent imprinting the accumulated wisdom of our culture is now spent creating and reinforcing a bogus and perfunctory "self-esteem."

There is a genuine crisis in education and public life over whether we really are a civilization and whether there is anything in the American past worth transmitting. In schools around the country, Thanksgiving and other national holidays that once bound us together have been transformed—with dreary uniformity—into "multicultural holidays," when children are asked to celebrate nothing more than their own ethnicity—and, by implication, their own egos.

This decay of our civilization was brought home to me in December 1992 when I was with Owen Roberts, a long-range-planning consultant in Tampa. That was when President Bush announced we were sending American troops to Somalia to save millions from starving to death. Owen was beside himself with anger at what he saw as a wasted opportunity. "We will temporarily stop the warlords," he exclaimed. "We will temporarily feed the people. Then we will leave and the situation will decay again because we will not have taught the Somalians the rule of law, the concept of self-reliance, the principles of free markets, or any of the conditions of a healthy self-governing country. What a waste!"

Without thinking I blurted, "If we don't teach ourselves how to be American anymore, why do you think we would teach other people?" What I said frightened me. The very things we weren't teaching the Somalians weren't going to be taught to poor Americans trapped in the welfare state. If Americans are not getting the lessons of America from their parents or from the educational system, where are they going to learn them?

This realization led me to the idea of teaching American Civilization as a form of self-improvement. The old adage, after all, is that the best way to learn is to teach. A key reason for teaching was to gain some hands-on experience in what it means to be passing on the values of American civilization. The biggest surprise was to find how far most twentieth-century intellectuals have strayed from the assumptions and values of the Founding Fathers.

Everett Carll Ladd, a leading student of American public opinion, was the first person to point this out to me. Ladd argues that America was built on the concepts of individual responsibility, the centrality of a Creator, and the sense of honor and duty that bound the Founding Fathers together. Just as the Creator has been driven from the public arena, so individual responsibility has been undermined by the philosophy of victimization and honor and duty have been replaced by cynicism and pleasure seeking. At Ladd's urging, I went back and read Henry Cabot Lodge's 1888 biography of George Washington. Although written in a different era, it told me more about America than many of today's well-researched volumes. As I read this forgotten work, I began to realize the degree to which America must be described in romantic terms. To take the romance out of America is to de-Americanize our own country. To me, America is a romance in which we all partake.

Gordon Wood's two great works, *The Creation of the American Republic* and *The Radicalism of the American Revolution*, further strengthened my understanding of the enormous gap between America as it was founded and America as it is being mistaught in academe. The Founding Fathers clearly understood that America was a new idea. They created a vision of self-government in which virtue and patriotism were primary safeguards of freedom's survival.

But this early "era of good feeling" did not last—nor should it have. By 1830, the rise of commercial society transformed America by extending more freedom and opportunity to everyone in the society except slaves. This was the Jacksonian revolution—a populist uprising of the increasing middle class that bears an uncanny resemblance to the upheavals we are undergoing today. As a result, America stabilized into a workable democratic culture just as de Tocqueville began his journeys in 1831, a journey that would eventually inform the world that "Democracy in America" worked.

As Wood observes, America in 1830 is as thoroughly recognizable as the America of the first half of the twentieth century, where mass tastes and a common popular culture prevailed. Even today, this democratic culture remains the common, everyday experience of nearly all Americans. This is the America of voluntary associations, practical problem solving, active local leadership, and an ethic of getting the job done as efficiently as possible. What is different today is that this practical, democratic culture has been overlaid with an elite culture—predominant in the upper echelons of Washington and the media—that says that American history is nothing but a story of racism, oppression, genocide, disenfranchisement, and constant violation of the norms to which we all thought we subscribed.

It is stunning to immerse yourself in the visionary world of the American experience—to listen, for example, to Lincoln raising cheers from white working-class audiences about Negro slaves' inherent right to keep the fruits of their own labor—and then to realize how much of this self-confidence and pride in our own accomplishments has been lost. We have gone from being a strong, self-reliant, vigorous society to a pessimistic one that celebrates soreheads and losers jealous of others' successes.

If you think I exaggerate, take a look at the speeches and letters of the Founding Fathers, of Lincoln, and of Theodore and Franklin Roosevelt and compare them with the querulous whining and petty grievances of so many modern columnists and academics today. I came out of my two years of reviewing American history convinced that our first need is to rediscover the values we have lost.

In my reading, I found five basic principles that I believe form the heart of our civilization:

1. The common understanding we share about who we are and how we came to be
2. The ethic of individual responsibility
3. The spirit of entrepreneurial free enterprise
4. The spirit of invention and discovery

5. Pragmatism and the concern for craft and excellence, as expressed most recently in the teachings of Edwards Deming

The history of who we are and how we came to be is especially important because we have grown as a people only out of our collective experience and memory. America is a series of romantic folktales that just happen to be true. We are a unique civilization. We stand on the shoulders of Western European civilization, but we are far more futuristic, more populist, and more inclusive. American civilization is not merely a subset of Western Europe's. We have drawn people and cultures from across the planet and integrated them into an extraordinary shared opportunity to pursue happiness.

The Spiritual Dimension

The fastest way to learn about America is by immersion in our history as a people and our emergence as a nation. From the Jamestown Colony and the Pilgrims to the very founding of the nation, the centrality of God and religion is unmistakable. All of our rights come from our Creator. Even today this is a very radical idea. In nearly all countries, power belongs to the state and is occasionally loaned to individuals. In America, power comes from God to the individual and is loaned to the state. It does not belong to the state or a king. It would be hard to imagine a greater difference in first principles.

Take just one historic example. When the Constitutional Convention was deadlocked and there was a real danger that the convention would break up over the fight between big and small states, Benjamin Franklin rose to calm tempers and restore to the delegates a common sense of purpose. His speech is instructive in recentering America on its relationship to God:

> In the situation of this Assembly, groping as it were in the dark to find political truth and scarce able to distinguish it

when presented to us, how has it happened, Sir, that we have not hitherto thought of humbly applying to the Father of Lights to illuminate our understandings? In the beginning of the contest with Great Britain, when we were sensible of the already great dangers we were only just entering, we held daily prayer in this room. Our prayers, Sir, were heard and graciously answered. All of us who were engaged in that struggle must have observed frequent instances of a superintending Providence in our favor. It is to that kind Providence that we owe this happy opportunity of consulting in peace on the establishment of our future national felicity.

And have we now forgotten that powerful Friend? Or do we imagine we no longer need His assistance? I have lived, Sir, a long time, and the longer I live, the more convinced I am of this truth—that God governs the affairs of men. And if a sparrow cannot fall to the ground without his notice, is it probable that an empire can rise without his aid? I believe, Sir, that "except the Lord Build the House, they that build it labor in vain." And I firmly believe that without His concurring aid we shall succeed in our task no better than the Builders of Babel. Our projects shall be confounded, and we ourselves shall become the reproach and byword of failure down through the age. What is worse, mankind may hereafter from this unfortunate instance despair of establishing a government by Human Wisdom and leave it instead to chance, war, and conquest.

The convention heeded Franklin's eloquent plea and shortly after was able to resolve its differences and complete the Constitution of the United States.

When the nation was faced with the scourge of slavery, those who argued that blacks could not legitimately be enslaved in a free country called again and again on the power of the Deity as a final witness to this judgment. Thomas Jefferson expressed it best when he said: "God who gave us life gave us liberty. Can the liberties of a nation be secure when we have removed a conviction that these liberties are the gift of God? Indeed I tremble for my country when I reflect that God is just, that his justice cannot sleep forever. Commerce between master and slave is despotism."

When the nation ultimately went to war over the issue, Abraham Lincoln called on the power and judgment of God in pressing the Union's cause. In his Second Inaugural Address, he wrote:

> If we shall suppose that American Slavery is one of those offenses which, in the providence of God, must needs come, but which, having continued through His appointed time, He now wills to remove, and that He gives to both North and South this terrible war, as the woe due to those by whom the offense came, shall we discern therein any departure from those divine attributes which the believers in a Living God always ascribe to Him? Fondly do we hope—fervently do we pray—that this mighty scourge of war may speedily pass away. Yet, if God wills that it continue, until all the wealth piled by the bondsman's two hundred and fifty years of unrequited toil shall be sunk, and until every drop of blood drawn with the lash, shall be paid by another drawn with the sword, as was said three thousand years ago, so still it must be said, "the judgments of the Lord are true and righteous altogether."

Eighty years later, when we were engaged in a struggle of equal magnitude with Nazi Germany, Franklin Delano Roosevelt, probably the greatest President of the twentieth century, openly appealed to the nation's sense of faith and religion in summoning the national will to the task. On the morning that the Allied armies invaded Normandy, President Roosevelt began a radio broadcast that was probably listened to by more than 80 percent of the American public. As historians have described it, "The world stood still" while people awaited the outcome of events at Omaha Beach.

With the attention of the entire nation riveted upon him, President Roosevelt did a remarkable thing. After telling the nation in one sentence that troops had landed, he said: "And so in this poignant hour, I ask you to join with me in prayer."

The President of the United States then spoke in the following fashion:

> Almighty God, our sons, pride of our nation, this day have set upon a mighty endeavor, a struggle to preserve our public, our religion, and our civilization and to set free a suffering humanity. Lead them straight and true, give strength to their arms, starkness to their hearts, steadfastness in their faith. They will need thy blessings.... Some will never return. Embrace these, Father, and receive them, thy heroic servants, into thy kingdom. And for us at home, fathers, mothers, children, wives, sisters, and brothers of brave men overseas, whose thoughts and prayers are ever with them, help us, almighty God, to rededicate ourselves in renewed faith in thee, in this hour of great sacrifice. Many people have urged that I call the nation into a single day of special prayer, but because the road is long and the desire is great, I ask that our people devote themselves in a continuance of prayer as we rise to each new day and again when each day is spent.... And Oh Lord, give us faith, faith in thee, faith in our sons, faith in each other, faith in our united crusade.... Thy will be done, Almighty God.

Ben Franklin, Thomas Jefferson, and Abraham Lincoln would have understood and approved.

What a sense of a Divine Order gives us is not the God of any one group's particular religion, but a sense that there is something larger than ourselves and our petty concerns of the day. Without a sense of faith, we become too embroiled in our own battles. The Americans who rebelled against English rule did not want to annihilate the British. They simply wanted to restore a balance of self-rule as Jefferson described so eloquently in the Declaration of Independence. Only when people lose sight of God do they seek "final solutions" to their problems.

Only when they have lost their sense of a larger humanity do they practice genocide.

We see similar extremes in some of our political debate. One of the most absurd of modern practices is the "war between men and women"—as if God didn't make us both male and female, as if both were not necessary for the propagation of the species. The same sense of something larger than today's newspaper headlines should govern our efforts to find peace between races and ethnic groups. What is at stake except the sense that we all carry a divine spark that makes us equals in the eyes of God?

America has never been a theocracy or a nation of saints. While God is central to our sense of national mission and destiny and personal faith is at the heart of the American experiment, we have also been a nation of sinners and sins. Only by immersing ourselves in our own history do we begin to pick up the rhythms of America and the simple themes that underlie the extraordinarily complex tapestry of its diverse peoples.

Individual Responsibility

Precisely because our rights are endowed by our Creator, the individual burden of responsibility borne by each citizen is greater than in any other country. This is why our new-found sense of entitlement and of victimization is exactly wrong—and so corrosive to the American spirit. In America, the fact that God, not the state, has empowered us puts an enormous burden on our shoulders. Our rights are pale shadows of our responsibilities. When the Founding Fathers pledged their lives, their fortunes, and their sacred honor they meant it literally. The consequence of defeat would be an ignoble hanging. Compare that level of personal commitment and self-assumed responsibility with the self-pity of the whiners we so often hear today.

One of the most important concepts of the countercultural left is the idea of an all-powerful "society." In their view "society" is always responsible for everything. If people murder and rape, it isn't their fault, it's the fault of "society." If teenage girls become pregnant almost as soon as they reach puberty, it isn't their own or their boyfriends' or their parents' fault, it's the fault of "society." If children don't learn and schools can't teach, it isn't some identifiable flaw in our educational system, it's just the fault of "society."

By blaming everything on "society," contemporary liberals are really trying to escape the personal responsibility that comes with being an American. If "society" is responsible for everything, then no one is *personally* responsible for anything. We can all blame one another and that's the end of it. To be an American, however, is to be responsible—both for yourself and, as much as possible, for others. When confronted with a problem, a true American doesn't ask, "Who can I blame this on?" A true American asks, "What can I do about it *today?*"

This brings us to another American characteristic: the work ethic. Captain John Smith's 1607 statement, "If you don't work you won't eat," is the complete opposite of today's redistribution ethic that subsidizes idleness. Nothing could be less traditionally American than the modern welfare system. It violates the American ethic that everyone should work hard to improve both their own lives and the lives of their children. If you are not prepared to shoulder personal responsibility, then you are not prepared to participate in American civilization.

The classic American is an independent, self-reliant, hardworking, honest person of no great wealth or social status who nonetheless has good sense, great courage, and a fierce love of country.

Joshua Chamberlain was a college professor at Bowdoin when he enlisted in the Civil War because he thought it was right to free the slaves and save the Union. Although he had no military experience, his uncommon good sense led him to rise quickly through the ranks. By Gettysburg, he was a colonel.

In the movie *Gettysburg,* Chamberlain is seen giving a speech to a group of Maine volunteers who have fulfilled the term of their enlistment and want to go home. He tells them in simple language that although most wars have been fought by men who had no real interest in the outcome, they are privileged in that they have the chance to fight for something that is right. In the end, the Maine regiment decides to stay and eventually defeats a key flanking attack that helps to determine the outcome of the battle. These events are not fiction. They really happened.

General George Marshall led with the same spirit in World War II. From his years as an infantry officer, Marshall knew that Americans were very poor at *taking* orders but would fight better than anyone if they *understood* why they were fighting. For this reason, he always insisted on keeping his troops informed and aware of the big picture. As a result, most historians now agree, by the end of World War II the American army was a vastly more powerful fighting force than the German army, even though the German army was a more professional unit that had been fighting for a longer time.

Dr. Martin Luther King, Jr., was a preacher who became imbued with the conviction that the Declaration of Independence meant it when it stated, "*All* men are created equal." His "army" was nothing more than a band of citizen-soldiers who had never participated in public life (they weren't even allowed to vote) but who were equally convinced that what they were doing was right. Marching under a banner of nonviolence, they aroused the national conscience and brought down an oppressive system of racial segregation. What motivated Dr. King was not a thirst for revenge, but an exalted effort to restore the balance between the rights granted by the Creator and the personal responsibilities that come with them. Old-time segregationists used to argue that blacks couldn't be granted the rights of citizens because they weren't capable of the personal responsibilities that went with them. Dr. King proved them wrong. That is why he triumphed and segregation ended.

Without personal responsibility there cannot be freedom. It is just that simple.

The Spirit of Free Enterprise

Americans get up every day hoping to put in a good day's work, create a little more wealth, provide a little better service to their customers, or invent a slightly better mousetrap for the world. From our founding we have been an astonishingly entrepreneurial society. People from every walk of life have embraced the dream that, given the opportunity, all individuals will be able to create a better future for themselves, their family, their community, and their country.

Part of the American genius has been that, at every level of society, people can improve their own lot. We have no caste system, no class requirements, no regulated professions, no barriers to entry. Despite the best efforts of modern elites to discount upward mobility and to argue that America is no different than Europe or other class-dominated cultures, the fact remains that we are an extraordinarily fluid society. In France, for example, almost all important government positions are held by graduates of the École Nationale d'Administration, an elite college that produces only a few graduates each year. In this country, Harvard's Kennedy School of Government might aspire to a similar status. But our society is so fluid and democratic that seven of our last ten Presidents did not attend elite colleges. Even a professor from a small college in Georgia can aspire to the highest levels of government.

It is no accident that Bill Gates, who founded Microsoft, and Steve Jobs, who cofounded Apple Computer, were both college dropouts. It is no accident that Thomas Edison, who never even finished high school, could invent so many products that by 1930 one of six jobs in the economy was derived from his life's work. It is no accident that Henry Ford, working in the daytime as chief mechanic at a Detroit Edison plant, could come home at night and build the automobile prototype in his garage that would make him one of the world's wealthiest men.

Vision, energy, ambition, hard work, dreaming of a better

future and then making it come true—these are the hallmarks of American entrepreneurialism. Edison described it perfectly when he said: "Genius is one per cent inspiration and ninety-nine per cent perspiration." He tried 4,000 different experiments with metals and alloys while trying to invent a durable storage battery. None of them worked. When someone asked him if he was discouraged by so much failure, he replied, "Those aren't failures. Those are 4,000 things we know don't work." More than 45,000 experiments later he hit upon the lead-acid storage battery and we have been using it ever since.

In the 1950s, John Kenneth Galbraith, the favorite economist of modern liberals, was writing that "All the simple, important inventions have already been made." The golden age of American enterprise was over, Galbraith argued, and there was nothing left to do but give government our wealth and let the politicians divide it up. How wrong he proved to be.

One favorite argument in the decline-of-America scenario is that all-important manufacturing jobs are declining and being replaced by unimportant service jobs. We may be giving people work, the argument goes, but it's nothing more than "hamburger flipping."

In response, I would advise these people to read *Grinding It Out,* the autobiography of Ray Kroc, founder of McDonald's. Kroc began his career in California as a milkshake machine salesman. He spotted a small restaurant in Bakersfield run by the McDonald brothers that seemed to have an extraordinarily strong following. Kroc urged the brothers to franchise their restaurant—mainly because he wanted to sell more milkshake machines. But the brothers weren't interested. So he finally persuaded them to lease him the name. Borrowing the McDonald's formula of a small menu with fast service, he opened his first McDonald's in Chicago. The rest is history.

Incidentally, when Kroc was opening the Chicago store he didn't have the money to install a soft-drink fountain. So the local

Coke salesman *gave* him a machine, hoping for future accounts. Because of that act of generosity and trust, McDonald's is now Coca-Cola's largest customer in the world.

Generosity, trust, optimism, and hard work—these are the elements that have driven the American entrepreneurial system, creating the most powerful and vibrant economy the world has ever known. Unfortunately, it isn't as easy as it used to be. Taxes, regulation, and litigation have all thrown a blanket over the entrepreneurial spirit. Elite criticisms of the can-do spirit have undermined that ethic. Credentialing of the professions has raised barriers to entrepreneurial inventiveness. The welfare system has sapped the spirit of the poor and made it harder to climb the first rungs of the economic ladder.

Despite these impediments, the spirit of free enterprise remains at the heart of American civilization. We need to comb through our educational system and laws to clean out the barriers to starting businesses and creating new wealth. We need to alter tax codes that virtually punish people for working as independent contractors or starting their own businesses. We need to change state and federal laws that give huge advantages to unionized employees of giant corporations and force small businesses and self-employed people to make up the difference. We must clear a path for the next Tom Edison or Ray Kroc. New Bill Gateses and Steve Jobses must be able to emerge from the black and Hispanic communities.

The lesson of American civilization is that inventing new forms of wealth is the key to a better future.

The Spirit of Invention and Discovery

More than any other country in history America has been committed to the spirit of invention and discovery. Part of this came from the very newness of the continent seen by the European settlers. Every day brought new discoveries. The newness of

America and its distance from Europe led to a spirit of practical local inventiveness that produced an explosion of new products and new ideas.

From Robert Fulton's steam engine (and his little-known submarine) to Eli Whitney's cotton gin (and his even more significant mass production of standardized parts), from Samuel Morse's invention of the telegraph (in a congressionally subsidized effort to link Washington and Baltimore) to the Wright brothers' invention of the airplane, America has had a remarkable history of new people pursuing new ideas without worrying much about the risks or what the last generation's received opinion might be.

Silicon Valley is a classic American example of how new people can create a whole new industry without credentials or official sanction. The number of shoestring operations and back-yard-garage inventions that have ultimately succeeded is astounding. The rise of molecular medicine is another example of American drive and energy chasing new ideas wherever they may lead.

Whether displaying determination on the battlefield, persistence in pursuing new inventions, or dedication in spending long, hard hours making an invention or dream come true, American individualism has been an enormously powerful force for good.

Pragmatism and the Spirit of Quality Taught by Deming

Edwards Deming is not a name familiar to most Americans. But he embodies so many of the traits of the American character that he deserves a place in the nation's mythology. He is already honored in Japan, where the highest annual award bestowed upon a Japanese company each year is the Deming Award for Quality.

Edwards Deming was born in 1900 and raised in Cody, Wyoming, a son of pioneers. He spent his young life on what was still very much the frontier. He became a successful business student and in the 1920s worked for AT&T, where he developed many of his ideas about human productivity. Deming was fortunate to be a young statistician working in the shadow of William Shewhart and participating in the classic Hawthorne experiment at the Western Electric plant during the 1920s.

At the time, the prevailing theory of assembly-line management was Taylorism, named for Frederick Winslow Taylor, who developed it at the turn of the century. Taylor did "time and motion studies" and broke down each step of an assembly line to its smallest part. A worker was fit into each of these parts. Consequently, assembly-line workers found themselves doing the same task day after day. They "hung their brains at the door" and did the minute task assigned them by management, as if they were automatons themselves.

Shewhart and Deming went to Hawthorne with the idea of improving the assembly line. Soon they discovered an interesting effect. If they increased the lighting, productivity improved. If they dimmed the lighting, productivity also improved. It was all very puzzling until the experimenters realized that lighting was not the problem. It was the *attention paid to the workers* that was improving productivity. Workers were subconsciously motivated to perform better because important people were looking at what they did.

The Shewhart-Deming approach of looking at workers' motivations spread. In World War II it was widely taught to production engineers and designers. The great explosion of American military productivity after Pearl Harbor was in no small part a tribute to their approach.

After the war, however, the Deming approach of rigorous statistical analysis and quality control disappeared from much of American industry. We had won the war. Our competitors had disappeared through the ravages of that great conflict. Everything we could produce could be sold. We did not have to focus on intense and difficult management systems. We could focus simply on mass production.

In 1950 Edwards Deming went to Japan at the invitation of its leading industrialists and government officials. In two brief days, he outlined his theories to a collection of Japan's top industrial executives. The Japanese were desperate to improve their economy. They knew that people around the world regarded their products as inferior imitations. They had heard a lot about the great American system of production (and had experienced its impact in the war) and wanted to learn how to produce quality products in great numbers. They had been told that Deming knew the secret to being as good as General Motors or Ford.

Deming later told me that 80 percent of Japan's industrial capital was in the room for those two days. He taught them a common set of ideas, language, and systems that became the hallmark of Japanese productivity. The idea of making high standards of quality the center of industrial production gradually disseminated into Japanese society. That is why the annual award for the best company in Japan is the Deming Award for Quality.

For thirty years American management shrugged off Deming's theories while Japan adopted them as a national standard. Finally, in the 1970s, it became obvious that Japanese manufacturing techniques had surpassed American mass production in many ways. American managers realized they had better find out what Deming was talking about. As Donald Petersen shows in *A Better Idea*, the subsequent turnaround by companies such as Ford has been due largely to the application of Deming's ideas.

My wife, Marianne, and I first learned about Deming's work at an annual senior management retreat of the Milliken Corporation, the nation's leading textile firm. Roger Milliken, a very imposing man, has been president since 1948 and is the company's largest stockholder.

The process of the Milliken management frankly shocked my wife and me. Although the company has a distinct hierarchy, information was allowed to percolate from the ground up. At the retreat I watched a thirty-eight-year-old sales manager engage Roger Milliken in a face-to-face debate and tell him in front of forty other people that he was wrong. When a junior executive born four years after the owner became president can speak with such temerity and still keep his job, there is clearly a different corporate culture at work.

At the Milliken retreat, Marianne and I were introduced to the "red bead game," a demonstration that Deming invented to prove his points about worker participation and quality control. The leader of the game invites members of his audience to participate in a typical "manufacturing process." A group of white beads, sprinkled with a few red beads, falls into a tray every thirty seconds. The red beads are the "defective products," and the job of the workers is to remove them. The system makes individual effort irrelevant. On average, though, with a group of four or five people, about fifteen red beads will always be left in the tray.

The leader then invites participants to invent various "management strategies" to improve performance. Workers are given bonuses for removing more beads. They are fired for removing too few beads. They are exhorted, encouraged, yelled at, dismissed—yet despite little blips here and there their performance never seems to improve. Since the system remains random, the results remain random. Individual effort is defeated by the system.

What the participants almost never do is challenge the whole design of the process. "Why are we removing these beads in the first place?" "Isn't there some better way to do this?" "Why not try removing the beads *before* they get in the tray?" All the inventiveness and ingenuity of the worker are ignored in the process. Because workers are never told what they are doing, they never bother to make suggestions. Because they are *assumed* to be stupid, they follow orders and never apply their intelligence to the problem.

Deming argued that in order to improve quality *everybody* has to get involved in designing and improving a manufacturing process, and they have to improve the system. No longer can workers be passive participants. Today this is called "total quality management" and has become increasingly prevalent in American industries. There are Ford plants in America today where, if you have a better idea for improving an assembly-line process, you will be flown immediately to Detroit to discuss it with top management.

With Milliken's encouragement, Marianne and I were drawn to Deming's theories of quality control and "profound knowledge." Owen Roberts, our chief adviser on long-range planning, then arranged for Marianne and me to meet Dr. Deming. I spent about sixty hours in a tutorial with him and Marianne took a fifty-hour course. Dr. Deming was in his early nineties at that point. Not only did he have the energy to teach ten hours a day, but Marianne found herself invited to his suite in the evening with a few other students to have hot chocolate and talk about ideas. He continued to teach every day until his death at ninety-three.

Although Deming's work defies any easy summary, his teachings generally focus around four basic points:

1. The customer should be the focus of any business. The producer must realize what the customer really wants—even if the customer doesn't realize it himself. Innovations such as the microwave oven, the fax, and the overnight delivery system all began as responses to needs that customers had not yet imagined or articulated. Yet, once invented, customers responded and they immediately became indispensable to millions.
2. Systems, rather than individuals, should be the focus of improving production. People are not the problem (unless they are willfully destructive). If production seems difficult to improve, it is not because the individuals are not functioning properly but because the whole system is ill conceived and has to be rethought and redesigned.
3. There has to be a theory or hypothesis before each change

or action. Prediction is the key to management. If you
don't have a theory to explain what you are doing, how can
you hope to improve the system?
4. Every employee can be a key player in improving a process
or product. Employees should be treated as knowledgeable
contributors to their activities. When management listens
to what workers have to say, the whole process will be
improved. Moreover, as workers realize they are being listened to, their contribution will increase dramatically.

The more I listened to Dr. Deming, the more I realized he
was classically American. Deming was imbued with the work
ethic, the sense of fair play, the belief that every person has
something to contribute. His passion grew out of his belief that
America was losing the race for productivity and that American
civilization was entering a period of economic decline.
Management leadership, he said, was refusing to learn the rules
of the Information Age. One of the reasons I decided to teach a
course on Renewing American Civilization and write a book on
renewing America was to propagate his thought. Deming can be
understood only within the values that are at the core of the
American experiment.

Government today works on the same 1920s Taylorite model
that has long been superseded in business. What we need now,
throughout the federal government, is the same sort of strategic
downsizing and overhaul of basic assumptions, based on respect
for individual achievement, that has benefited businesses so
enormously in the past decade.

The best tribute we can give Dr. Deming is to reestablish
America as a country in which every citizen has an opportunity
to contribute his or her share to the fullest of his or her abilities.
That will be a renewal of American values and a true fulfillment
of Deming's American dream.

CHAPTER 4

America and the Third Wave Information Age

Just list some of the changes we are living through: laptop computers, cellular telephones, molecular medicine, new discoveries about the dinosaurs, home security systems that talk, composite materials that make cars lighter, microengineering, manufacturing in space, high-definition television, the video store—the list goes on and on. If we were to spend just one week itemizing everything we encounter that our grandparents would not have believed, we would be astonished at the totality of change we are living through.

My aunt Loma gave me a vivid illustration of living through large-scale change when she described her one experience in learning how to drive a car. Aunt Loma was born in 1898 in a mountainous part of Pennsylvania, about forty miles south of State College. Her family worked hard on a poor but comfortable farm. When she married Uncle Cal, she was perfectly content to have him drive. In 1928 he finally convinced her she should try it. "We went out into a large field. I told him I didn't want to drive but he insisted I try. I got behind the wheel and put my foot on the gas. He started yelling something about the brakes but I froze and couldn't do anything. We hit a fence at about fifteen miles an hour. I got out and said, 'There, I have tried.'" And that was that. She lived to age ninety-four, relying on buses and letting others tackle newfangled skills.

People faced with laptop computers, Internet connections, cellular phones, and the possibility of space travel often take Aunt Loma's attitude. If you try to deal with it all, you can get overwhelmed. That was the message of Alvin and Heidi Toffler's first bestseller, *Future Shock*, in which they addressed the pace of change in modern life. If people became overwhelmed with change, said the Tofflers, they could go into a state of dejection and exhaustion.

A decade later, the Tofflers wrote a more sophisticated analysis, which they said could minimize confusion and help people like Aunt Loma understand and adjust to the scale of change we are experiencing. They described our era as the Third Wave of change.

In the Tofflers' view—with which I agree—the transformation we are experiencing is so large and historic that it can be compared with only two other great eras of human history—the Agricultural Revolution and the Industrial Revolution. The Agricultural Revolution—the "First Wave"—occurred when hunting-and-gathering tribes first invented agriculture. Through the earliest part of human history, tribes of twenty to thirty nomads crossed the landscape following game herds (similar to the life of Kalahari Bushmen or Australian Aborigines today). Within a few millennia, these tribes had switched to a densely populated world of six million farmers staying in one place and growing a small number of very productive crops. This First Wave was actually the largest population explosion in human history. The population in Egypt increased three hundred-fold (30,000 percent) during the transition from hunting and gathering to farming. There had never been anything else like it. Suddenly people could accumulate goods over several generations. People became skilled in crafts like carpentry and wagonmaking. Traditions and hierarchies were established. Governments, priesthoods, kingships, armies, and tax collectors appeared.

Imagine trying to tell a hunter-gatherer what the world would be like after the Agricultural Revolution. Imagine trying to tell someone living in a small band that he or she would live in a fixed place surrounded by thousands of people. Imagine telling someone who has hunted over scores of square miles for an occasional large animal that he or she might live among herds of sheep, cows, goats, and camels. It would be difficult if not impossible.

All classic civilizations—Rome, Greece, China, the Indus Valley, Egypt, Babylon, the Inca-Mayan and Aztec civilizations of the Americas—resulted from the Agricultural Revolution. This wave carries us through all of ancient and medieval history. George Washington could have conversed easily with Julius Caesar. Both rode on horseback, relied on sailing ships, and wrote with quill pens. Both relied on ox-drawn carts to supply their armies. Caesar's transport problems in Gaul and Washington's at Valley Forge were essentially the same.

Then, a second wave of change occurred at the start of the eighteenth century. Beginning in Britain and rapidly spreading to Western Europe and America, the development of power-driven industry created another wave of productivity, wealth, and power that transformed people's lives.

In the agricultural era, 97 percent of all workers were engaged in farming. Each produced a tiny surplus. Large systems of government and elites were sustained by gathering together the surpluses from thousands and thousands of small farms. This model remained true everywhere in the agricultural world.

The Second Wave changed all the economic equations. Imagine trying to explain to a resident of Rome or the Middle Ages a world in which only three percent of the work force would be engaged in farming. Imagine further trying to explain that a major side effect would be large agricultural surpluses. Rather than starving to death, people will be overweight and worry about eating too much food. Even under these conditions, farmers will be too productive and every industrial government will have to subsidize them.

When Malthus wrote his dire prediction of overpopulation and mass starvation, the industrial transformation of farming had just begun. At the time, Britain and most other countries were trying to be self-sufficient. Within a few decades, liberalized trade laws allowed Britain to import enormous amounts of food at lower cost. As a result, Great Britain today has a population eleven times the size that Malthus said it could not support.

The Second Wave caused another great discontinuity—only this time at a much more rapid pace. While George Washington could have chatted easily with Julius Caesar, he would have had a difficult time talking with Theodore Roosevelt. While Teddy was President, the mass-produced automobile, the full-length motion picture, and the airplane made their debut—all in one year, 1903. Electric lights were becoming common, streetcars were standard transportation, telephones were more and more available. Roosevelt—who embraced these changes enthusiastically—became the first President to ride in a car and was praised by newspapers for the courage he displayed in doing so.

Now we are entering a third great era of change, the transformation from the Industrial Age to the Information Age. Breakthroughs like computers, worldwide electronic transmissions, satellites, fiber optics, molecular biology, and a host of others are making life vastly different.

One of the great problems people have in entering an era of change is nostalgia for the passing era. People feel a sense of quiet despair in watching an old era end. During the industrial transformation, writers like H. G. Wells and Jules Verne emerged to give the new era an aura of excitement.

One individual in our era who was willing to do the same is Ronald Reagan. He had made a career out of technology, moving from commercial radio (which did not exist when he was born) to movies and television, and then to working for General Electric ("Progress is our most important product"). Reagan always saw the potential of new technologies to improve the lives of ordinary people. His favorite line—"You ain't seen nothing yet"—expressed that optimism.

The coming of the Third Wave Information Age brings potential for enormous improvement in the lifestyle choices of most Americans. There is every reason to believe that this new era will see a revolution in goods and services that will empower and enhance most people.

Imagine a morning in just a decade or so. You wake up to a wall-size, high-definition television showing surf off Maui. (This is my favorite island—you can pick your own scene.) You walk or jog or do Stairmaster while catching up on the morning news and beginning to review your day's schedule. Your home office is filled with communications devices, so you can ignore rush-hour traffic. In fact, since most Americans now telecommute, rush hour is dramatically smaller than it used to be. Telecommuting has proved to be the best means of dealing with air pollution.

When you are sick, you sit in your diagnostic chair and communicate with the local health clinic. Sensors take your blood pressure, analyze a blood sample, or do throat cultures. The results are quickly relayed to health aides, who make recommendations and prescribe medicine. The only time you visit a doctor or hospital is when something is seriously wrong. If you need a specialist, a databank at your fingertips gives you a range of choices based on cost, reputation, and outcome patterns. You can choose knowledgeably which risk you want to take and what price you want to pay. If you face some rare or life-threatening disease, information systems will allow you to study the most advanced work around the world—things that even your doctor is unlikely to know. Because information is now so widely available, the guildlike hold of the medical profession has been broken. Health care has become more flexible and convenient—and less expensive.

Your legal problems will work the same way. You can write your own will, file your own adoption papers, form your own partnership or corporation—all with software programs available in your home. Then you e-mail them to the proper authorities. Any disciplined and educated person can now "read the law." Once again, the "legal guild"—so similar to the medieval craft guilds that were scattered by the Industrial Revolution—has been broken. People now bring their own lawsuits, file their own briefs, even represent themselves electronically in court. This democratization of the law—plus the astonishing decline in government regulation—has drastically reduced the demand for professionals. Fortunately, since most lawyers were reasonably smart and well-educated people, they have been able to find other lines of work.

Now imagine you want to learn something new, solve a personal problem, or enter some new profession. Do you have to go to night school or trek twenty-five miles to the nearest college? No, you simply enter the on-line learning system and describe what you need. Say you want to learn batik because a new craft shop has opened at the mall and the owner has told you she will sell some of your work. First, you check in at the "batik station" on the Internet, which gives you a list of recommendations. You can look through dozens of references. The Internet is like a library in which the books are never off the shelves. You may get a list of recommended video or audio tapes that can be delivered to your door the next day by Federal Express. You may prefer a more personal learning system and seek an apprenticeship with the nearest batik master, or you may want to take a traditional course offered at a local college or school. In less than twenty-four hours, you can launch yourself on a new profession. In a society of continuous, lifelong learning, these options will be available to everyone.

Living in a world that is bathed in information—too much information for any one person or company to absorb—your livelihood and security are likely to come from becoming an expert—maybe the world's greatest expert—on one small corner of this vast infosphere. You may become the foremost authority on some obscure medical procedure or accounting principle. You may know more than anyone else about the incorporation laws of Zaire and offer advice to anyone attempting to set up a business in that country. This is the way most professional consultants and small businesses operate now, and the way all businesses are now going. Corporate giants are finding it just doesn't make sense anymore to try to bring all their expertise under one roof. It's much easier to "outsource," relying on small, mobile, independent contractors for information. The world of information these companies must master is exploding.

This means that more and more people are going to be operating *outside* corporate structures and hierarchies in the nooks and crannies that the Information Revolution creates. While the Industrial Revolution herded people into gigantic social institutions—big corporations, big unions, big government—the Information Revolution is breaking up these giants and leading us back to something that is—strangely enough—much more like de Tocqueville's 1830s America.

The rhythm of the Third Wave Information Age will be a bit like rafting down the rapids after we have learned to canoe on a quiet lake. Although rafting may be more difficult or dangerous, the skills and conventions are essentially the same. Once we get adjusted, it can even be exhilarating. There are many more challenges, much more excitement, and our skills are honed to a much finer degree. There will be a lot more challenges in our new world than in the one we grew up in. During the transition, however, people are likely to be uncertain and intimidated.

There will also be enormous advantages for America and Americans if we lead the world in the transition to the Third Wave Information Age. Just as Britain profited enormously by leading the world into the industrial era, so the United States can profit enormously by being the leader in the development of the new goods, services, systems, and standards associated with a technological revolution of this scale.

Bill Loughrey of Scientific Atlanta has developed a good example of the scale of change we are living through. He notes that the advance from the vacuum tube to the transistor to the computer chip has resulted in a million-fold improvement in productivity over the last forty years. The power of computer chips will multiply another million-fold over the next ten years—as big an increase as the productivity improvement of the last forty years. This translates into a one-trillion-fold increase in productivity between 1950 and 2000.

Loughrey then draws a parallel with the failure of improvement in the federal government. If the federal government had improved at the same pace as the computer chip, he notes wryly, it would only have four employees and a total budget of $100,000. While Loughrey is clearly being facetious, there is an enormous truth to this analogy.

Almost every time I make a speech, I pull out a vacuum tube (technically an argon gas electron tube) that is still a key component in our federal air traffic control system. The tube was originally developed in 1895 and represents solid nineteenth-century technology. As the ranking Republican on the House Aviation Subcommittee almost a decade ago, I found that the Federal Aviation Commission was trying to replace this tube with computer chips. You can understand why. A computer chip I show that is almost too small to be seen on camera has the processing power of *three million* vacuum tubes. The United States has even started poking around Eastern Europe for supplies because few companies in the West make them anymore. Yet in the seven years since I first sat on the committee, the FAA has been unable to switch technologies. The United States government is now the largest remaining purchaser of vacuum-type tubes in the Western world.

Why are governments so painfully slow at adjusting to change? Why are their agencies almost always obsolete? The basic reason is that governments are not customer driven. Governments almost always grant monopoly status to their own operations so they won't have to compete. Look at public education. Look at the post office. It's the same story everywhere. Consumers are too often stuck with inefficient service and a poor product because they're not allowed to go anywhere else.

Because government operations don't have to please consumers, they end up catering to employees. That's why most government operations are overstaffed. Unionization has only made things worse. Almost 40 percent of government employees around the country are now members of labor unions. The figure for private industry is only 11 percent.

Change inconveniences employees, and that's why governments end up lagging in technology. Installing computers means employees have to learn new tasks. It's also likely to put a few people out of work—although ultimately it creates more jobs. Private corporations have been vigorous about restructuring and reengineering themselves over the last decade. That's why we've raced to the head of the pack again as the world's most efficient industrial nation. But government lags behind—often by decades, as the vacuum-tube illustration shows. Given the tough choice of restructuring with new technology or adding new employees to the same old tasks, government management will always choose the latter. It's much easier to swallow the costs and raise taxes.

The history of the United States has been a history of encouraging new developments and inventors. From Lewis and Clark's expedition to the Pacific Coast to John Wesley Powell's trip through the Grand Canyon, from Admiral Byrd's expeditions to the poles to Marsh's and Cope's hunts for fossils in the West, Americans have always relished discovery and adventure. At the same time, we were inventing practical solutions to everyday life—the sewing machine, the combine and harvester, barbed wire, and the zipper.

Not only have we been good at making our own discoveries,

we have also been energetic and aggressive at developing other countries' ideas. Marconi invented the radio in Italy, but the U.S. Navy put it into practice by encouraging the formation of the Radio Corporation of America (RCA). The internal combustion engine was a German invention, but its use in cars, trucks, and airplanes was pioneered in America. In Europe, inventions often remained the province of the wealthy and the aristocratic. In America, every young man and woman could aspire to participation in the creation of a new world.

The same spirit of democratic entrepreneurialism is alive in America today, but we do far less to encourage it. We have allowed mindless entertainment and liberal social issues to drive entrepreneurialism and invention from popular awareness.

We need to bring back to the center of the popular culture an intense awareness that the future is going to be very exciting and has the dramatic potential to improve everyone's life. We need to develop simple methods for people to participate eagerly and enthusiastically in inventing their own future.

The government needs to look at the changes in taxation, litigation, regulation, education, welfare, and government bureaucracies in order to encourage innovation and discovery. We need a series of commissions made up of entrepreneurs and inventors, plus citizen-customers and practitioners from the industrial-era guilds and professions. What should public safety be like in the Third Wave Information Age? How should a citizen-based health system be structured? What should lifetime learning be like? How could the legal system be simplified and made available to normal citizens without the cost of a lawyer? How could the government be remade to utilize the opportunities of the Information Age? We need a new sense of the opportunities that exist if only we have the courage to open our eyes and minds to them.

We are entering a revolutionary period in telecommunications when the regional "Baby Bells" will be able to compete with long-distance carriers, cable companies will compete with the regional Bells, and the power companies (who have the largest fiber optic network in the United States) may end up competing with everyone. This will be an amazingly complex communications system—a world apart from the black dial telephone of my childhood that was owned by the largest monopoly in the world.

In this world of instant and facile communication, why should schools have a monopoly on learning? Why should doctors and hospitals have a monopoly on practicing medicine? Why should lawyers have a monopoly on the legal profession? And why should all these industrial-era guilds and monopolies have their powers to coerce people protected by the government?

I am not advocating that we take drastic steps tomorrow morning, but I am advocating that we start asking bold and dramatic questions today. When we look around, we are surprised at how many goods and services are legally protected by the government. It is shocking how much protected professionals can charge when people have no choice but to go to them.

In *The Wealth of Nations*, Adam Smith describes brilliantly the impact of the emerging second wave industrial revolution on the medieval guilds. He notes that many groups, like weavers, tried to enlist the power of the state to stop new competitors (the textile mills) from putting them out of business. Smith's classic work became the foundation of modern market economics because he understood the dynamics of his changing era.

The same kind of changes are happening once again today. If we liberate entrepreneurs and make it relatively easy for them to discover and invent our new world, we will be rearing a generation that increases our wealth and improves our lives to a degree that we can now barely imagine.

CHAPTER 5

Creating American Jobs in the World Market

O ne of the great changes of the last twenty years has been the rise of the world market and the degree to which Americans feel threatened by the economic competition and economic uncertainties found there. Americans who had felt unchallengeable from 1945 to 1970 have increasingly felt not only challenged but at times unequal to the challenge of competitors around the world.

In part, this new sense of competitive reality is only natural. We came out of World War II with an unnatural and unsustainable sense of invulnerability. All of our major competitors had been bombed during the war, and there literally was no major competition to American industry. We then assumed an attitude of superiority that would get us into trouble in the 1970s, and from which our automobile industry, for example, took more than a decade to overcome.

We still face some severe disadvantages in competing in the world market. First, we ourselves are far and away the largest market in the world, and that makes it worth every other country's time and effort to compete here. But it is much harder for American companies elsewhere, particularly in small foreign countries whose economies are often smaller than those of, say, San Diego or Atlanta.

We have had such a powerful national economy for so long that it is difficult for us to adjust to the overwhelming realities of the world market. This is not just a business community problem. All current economics textbooks are based on the national economy as though that were still the keystone of an understanding of how the world works. Yet the fact is that the world economy is now, in large part, an interconnected system of electronic signals. When a twenty-eight-year-old English junior banker can risk over a billion dollars from a branch in Singapore, lose it in Tokyo, and thus bankrupt a venerable institution in London, it is clear that the world is changing. As one observer noted, when you lose the bank that financed the Louisiana Purchase in 1803, you know something noteworthy is going on.

Smaller countries have long felt the weight of the world economy. When the French Socialists in the early 1980s tried to develop their own economic policy without regard to what was going on in the rest of Europe, they were rapidly beaten into submission by monetary changes they found themselves powerless to resist. When the Japanese fatally overvalued their real estate and stock market, the crash was long and painful.

The long-term drop in the value of the dollar relative to the German mark and the Japanese yen is a warning to us that we too are tied into the same markets and bound by the same rules as everyone else. If we refuse to balance our budget over a long period of time, we will gradually undermine our currency. If we insist on taxation, litigation, and regulation that make us less competitive, we will gradually lose wealth to other countries. If our welfare system discourages work and our education system ignores homework, we will gradually lose our ability to compete worldwide in producing goods and services.

If we intend to give our children the best job security, the best quality of life, and the best take-home pay in the world, then we are going to have to rethink our entire approach to being competitive in the world market.

If we are serious about American success, we must begin by learning from our major multinational corporations under what circumstances they would create their next thousand high-value-added jobs in the United States. How do we need to change taxes, litigation, and regulation to make America a more desirable place to build the next factory, open the next laboratory, create the next design center? What changes in the education system are needed so young Americans can be more productive than their competitors and our companies can afford to provide sophisticated jobs here?

We also need to approach our major exporters and ask what help they need to compete in the world market. To what extent does the American tax code undermine American sales overseas? If we can create American jobs through world sales, how do we maximize world sales? In what ways can our government be more effective in making sure that American companies get an even break and that trade agreements are honored? To what extent does our government need to be tougher in compelling our trading partners to live up to their agreements? No matter how competitive we are economically, if we are being legally blocked from a market by the local government, we simply are not going to make any sales.

We also need to rethink America as a job and foreign exchange producer. Historically when we have thought of travel and tourism we have thought of Americans going overseas. Yet the United States is a terrific travel destination. We want to increase dramatically the number of visitors coming to the United States to spend their currency. Travel and tourism is the second largest industry in the world yet we still undervalue its potential as a job creator here in the United States. The rise of the cruiseline industry, based largely in Miami, which has created hundreds of thousands of jobs, is one indication of what tourism can mean. The impact of Disney World on the entire Orlando, Florida, area is another example of the powerful economic impact a vacation attraction can have.

Finally, we must aggressively explore the potential for massive job creation through Third Wave Information Age technologies. The American motion picture industry, with its use of new technologies and entrepreneurial creativity, is unsurpassed as a world competitor. In some countries 80 percent of all motion picture dollars go to American products. In computer software we have a similarly huge lead over our competitors. In computer chips we have regained the lead from Japan and seem to be pulling ahead. If we develop the same relative lead in biotechnology and health care we will see a massive influx of foreign exchange earnings.

No nation can lead the world if it can't economically sustain itself. Unless we accept our role as world leader, our planet will eventually be a dark and bloody place. No other nation is in a position to assume our mantle. We therefore have an absolute obligation to our children and grandchildren to commit ourselves to a strategy of winning the economic competition within the new world market.

There is also a practical, selfish reason for us to focus on being the most competitive economy in the world as we enter this new Third Wave Information Age. There will be an enormous opportunity for this country to develop the new products, the new wealth, the new jobs, and the new quality of life that will then transform both the lives of Americans and, over time, those of others. If we lead the economic and technological transition, then our children will have the highest-value-added jobs, with the highest productivity, with the highest take-home pay, the greatest job security, the widest choices in quality of life.

If we decide to relax, forget the hard work of reforming our system, and gradually decline into mediocrity, then our children will have poorer jobs with less job security and lower take-home pay. In that context our quality of life will be lower and our choices more narrow. That will also mean there will be fewer resources available for Social Security, for Medicare, for retiring baby boomers and their children.

The power of economic growth was driven home to me by a study that suggested that a 1 percent increase in our economic growth rate would shrink the federal deficit by $640 billion over the next seven years, would increase federal tax revenues by $716 billion *without a tax increase,* and that each and every adult citizen would earn $9,600 more than they would in the current growth projection.

In this world of merely 1 percent higher growth, the Social Security Trust Fund never runs out of money for as far as the current model can look into the future. By contrast, the current projection has the Social Security Trust Fund going into deficit by about 2029. If we have 1 percent less growth than projected, the Social Security Trust Fund goes into deficit thirteen years sooner, in 2016.

The power of economic growth to change our future both as individuals and as a country is one of my friend Jack Kemp's primary messages. He keeps trying to convince people that high growth rates can be achieved and sustained. High economic growth is a simple result of following the right policies, just as good health comes from good nutrition and exercise.

The so-called business cycle is in large part a product of the theories of American economists. Since their theories predict that economic recession will always follow growth, they will advise the Federal Reserve Board to follow policies that slow growth and increase interest rates, that in turn will choke off the growth and lead to a recession. This pattern may say more about American economists than it does about the American economy.

In Japan, where the government had a commitment to steady economic growth, there was a nineteen-year period without a recession. From 1975 to 1994 the Japanese averaged 4.2 percent annual growth and a 3.6 percent annual personal income increase. By contrast, in the same nineteen years the United States suffered through three recessions, the average annual growth rate was 1.6 percent lower (only 2.6 percent a year), and the annual personal income increase was 2.6 percent lower (only 1 percent a year for the nineteen-year period).

These numbers are not just of academic interest to financiers and economists. If the United States had grown at the same rate as Japan from 1975 to 1994, our real economy would have been $1.8 trillion bigger, our per capita income would have been $8,955 greater, and federal revenues would have been $393 billion higher. Our deficit would have turned into a surplus. We would be paying off our national debt by about $100 billion a year. The impact of a faster economic growth pattern is that dramatic.

Economic growth is the most important social policy objective a country can have other than keeping its people physically safe. Without economic growth there will be no jobs for current welfare recipients to go to when we reform the system. Without economic growth there will be no resources to sustain the Medicare system. Without economic growth the baby boomers will not be able to rely on their Social Security benefits. Without economic growth our children will not be able to earn enough to pay interest on the national debt, help pay for their parents' and grandparents' Social Security and Medicare, help pay for their own generation's government, help save for their own retirements, and still have some income to live on.

Economic growth is that central to a sound social policy for the whole country. When the pie is getting bigger everyone stays busy trying to cut a bigger piece for themselves and their families and neighbors. When the pie starts shrinking people begin to get selfish and jealous. The whole social fabric of the country is strained.

America's future depends on economic growth. Economic growth depends on our ability to compete in the world market.

Competing in the world market is going to require a lot of reforms, a lot of work, and a willingness to face reality and then be more creative, more energetic, and more optimistic than any of our competitors. We can do it. In fact, we have to do it. We owe it to our children and our country.

CHAPTER 6

Replacing the Welfare State with an Opportunity Society

The greatest moral imperative we face is replacing the welfare state with an opportunity society. For every day that we allow the current conditions to continue, we are condemning the poor—and particularly poor children—to being deprived of their basic rights as Americans. The welfare state reduces the poor from citizens to clients. It breaks up families, minimizes work incentives, blocks people from saving and acquiring property, and overshadows dreams of a promised future with a present despair born of poverty, violence, and hopelessness.

When a welfare mother in Wisconsin can be punished for sewing her daughter's clothing and saving on food stamps so she can set aside three thousand dollars for her daughter's education, you know there is something wrong.

When a woman who sells candy out of her apartment in a public housing project cannot open a store because she would lose her subsidized rent and health care and end up paying in taxes and lost benefits all she earned in profit, you know there is something wrong.

Gary Franks, congressman from Connecticut, tells of going into grade schools and asking young children what they hope to be when they grow up. Basketball players, football players, and baseball players are the three answers, in that order. What if you can't be an athlete? he then asks. They have no answer. It is beyond the experience of these children to consider becoming a lawyer or an accountant or a businessman. The public housing children, no matter what their ethnic backgrounds, have simply no conception of the world of everyday work. Clearly something is wrong.

Charlie Rangel, the senior congressman from Harlem, asked me to imagine what it would be like to visit a first- or second-grade classroom and realize that every fourth boy would be dead or in jail before he was twenty-five years old. As I think of my three nephews, Charlie's comment drives home to me the despair and rage at the heart of any black leader as he looks at the lost future of a generation of poor children. Clearly something is wrong.

The defenders of the status quo should be ashamed of themselves. The current system has trapped and ruined a whole generation while claiming to be compassionate. The burden of proof is not on the people who want to change welfare. It is on those who would defend a system that has clearly failed at incalculable human cost.

Consider the facts. Welfare spending is now $305 billion a year. Since 1965 we have spent $5 trillion on welfare—more than the cost of winning World War II. Yet despite this massive effort, conditions in most poor communities have grown measurably worse. Since 1970 the number of children living in poverty has increased by 40 percent. Since 1965 the juvenile arrest rate for violent crimes has tripled. Since 1960 the number of unmarried pregnant teenage girls has nearly doubled and teen suicide has more than tripled. As welfare spending increased since 1960, it has exactly paralleled the rise in births outside of marriage. On a graph, the two lines move together like a pair of railroad tracks. The more we spend to alleviate poverty, the more we assure that the next generation will almost certainly grow up in poverty. Clearly something is profoundly wrong.

We owe it to all young Americans in every neighborhood to save them from a system that is depriving them of their God-given rights to life, liberty, and the pursuit of happiness. There can't be true liberty while they are trapped in a welfare bureau-cracy. There can't be any pursuit of happiness when they are not allowed to buy property or accumulate savings. And there can't be any reasonable right to a long life in an environment that is saturated with pimps, prostitutes, drug dealers, and violence.

Make no mistake: replacing the welfare state will not be an easy job. It will not work simply to replace one or two elements while leaving everything else intact. It will be necessary to think through the entire process before we begin.

Replacing the welfare state with an opportunity society will require eight major changes, which need to be undertaken simul-taneously. Trying to change only one or two at a time will leave people trapped in the old order. We have an obligation to begin improving the lives of the poor from day one.

When people tell me I am intense on this issue, I ask them to imagine that their children were the ones dying on the evening news and then tell me how intense they would be to save their own children's lives. That is how intense we should all be.

One of the encouraging developments of the last few years has been that a lot of truly caring, intelligent people have spent a lot of time thinking about the tragedy of modern welfare systems. As a result, we now have a fairly good idea of what works and what doesn't. The eight steps we need for improving opportunities for the poor are:

1. Shifting from caretaking to caring
2. Volunteerism and spiritual renewal
3. Reasserting the values of American civilization
4. Emphasizing family and work
5. Creating tax incentives for work, investment, and entrepreneurship
6. Reestablishing savings and property ownership
7. Learning as the focus of education
8. Protection against violence and drugs

Let us consider each one of these in turn.

1. Shifting from Caretaking to Caring

In *Working Without a Net*, Morris Schechtman emphasizes the distinction between (1) caretaking—a more casual attitude, in which the important concern is to make the provider feel good, no matter what the outcome and (2) caring—a more selfless but positive approach, in which the outcome for the person being helped is the first concern. Caretaking has established the Supplemental Security Income (SSI) system, which has allowed, for example, forty disabled alcoholics to have their government checks registered directly at a Denver liquor store. Caring, on the other hand, would require any poor or disabled person to be partners in their own self-improvement.

The distinction between the deserving and the undeserving poor is at the heart of Marvin Olasky's great book, *The Tragedy of American Compassion*. Olasky emphasizes that indiscriminate aid actually destroys people. In addition, the sight of undeserving people getting resources while refusing to be responsible for themselves sends a devastating message to those working poor who are trying to make the effort to improve their lot. Besides undermining individual morality, indiscriminate aid undermines society as a whole.

From Colonial times until the 1960s, Olasky argues, American reformers made a clear distinction between poverty, a condition in which an individual or family did not have much money but their morality had not been undermined, and pauperism, a condition of passive dependency in which the work ethic has been completely lost. Social reformers emphasized that nothing could be more destructive than giving people help they didn't deserve. These experienced, traditional reformers saw as the most dangerous person the wealthy caretaker who passed out money to make himself feel good even as it ruined people in the process.

Olasky's model for true caring requires a level of detailed knowledge that is not possible for government bureaucracies. Because of the very magnitude of the task they attempt to undertake, government caretakers can do nothing more than provide indiscriminate handouts for income maintenance.

2. Volunteerism and Spiritual Renewal

In the nineteenth century, Olasky notes, there was an average of one volunteer for every two poor people. Under these circumstances, volunteers could actually get to know individuals and their families and could trace whether they were making progress. It takes detailed knowledge to assess what people and their families need. The resulting system emphasized both volunteerism and spiritual salvation.

Olasky cites again and again the difference between trying to maintain people in poverty, alcoholism, and addiction and helping them rise above their circumstances. Maintenance programs will eventually attract more people into the kind of pauperism we are trying to avoid than it will help escape from poverty. This was the consistent concern of nineteenth-century reformers, and we now have more than enough evidence to prove they were right.

Olasky also cites the role of spiritual transformation in saving people from poverty. Unless people get some kind of religious bearings, it is unlikely they will make the effort needed to change their circumstances. It is no accident that Alcoholics Anonymous gives God a central place in any effort to recover from addiction. For two generations we have tried to replace spiritual transformation with secular counseling. The experiment has failed miserably. Since no secular bureaucracy can (or should) engage in spiritual renewal, it is clear this effort must be undertaken by churches, synagogues, mosques, or other charitable and nonprofit institutions.

Congressmen Jim Kolbe and Joe Knollenberg have come up with a stunning suggestion for transforming welfare. Instead of the government taking billions of dollars from reluctant taxpayers and scattering it among the poor, individual taxpayers would be allowed to check off contributions of up to one hundred dollars for donation to their favorite charity—just as you are now allowed to check off three dollars for the Presidential Election Campaign Fund. This would shift $9 billion a year into private organizations offering spiritual help. It would also give taxpayers some control over how their money is being spent. Taxpayers would be able to vote with their checkbooks if a charitable effort were having counterproductive results.

I am proud to work with Habitat for Humanity, which helps poor people build their own homes. Millard and Linda Fuller founded Habitat after becoming convinced that a spiritually based approach was necessary to help the poor. Habitat screens families to find people who they believe deserve help (something the government cannot do). Those who are chosen are required to take a twenty-four-hour course on how to be a homeowner (something that HUD's lawyers say cannot be required). Habitat first asks the family to invest one hundred hours of sweat equity in helping build someone else's house and then three hundred hours in building their own home. Finally, Habitat sells them a $70,000 house for $36,000 with the understanding that if they try to sell it before the mortgage is paid off, they will have to pay off a second mortgage that covers the whole price of the home.

Volunteers like myself also come on Saturdays to work on the projects. It is a rewarding experience to see the future homeowning family there alongside public-spirited citizens. Habitat for Humanity is a program that combines prayer with practical help, a model for volunteerism and spiritual renewal of the kind Olasky writes about. That is why I wear a Habitat pin on my lapel.

3. Reasserting the Values of American Civilization

Every day on television and radio poor people see and hear things that reinforce the message that income transfer is what matters and spiritual transformation is unimportant. In her great book *The Demoralization of Society*, Gertrude Himmelfarb argues that the values and attitudes people have about themselves depend on the messages the culture sends them. She also notes that these attitudes can change in a very short period of time.

I believe we are at the end of the era of tolerating alcoholism, addiction, spouse and child abuse, parental indifference, and adult irresponsibility. We have all seen society change for the better in recent years in its views on smoking, drunk driving, and racism. There is no reason that views on acceptable standards of behavior for the poor cannot change as well.

When I spoke in March 1995 to the National League of Cities, I cited Himmelfarb's book and asserted that the time had come to reestablish shame as a means of enforcing proper behavior. It is shameful, I said, to be a public drunk at three in the afternoon and we ought to say so. People began applauding. It is shameful, I said, for males to have children they refuse to support and we ought to say so. The applause grew louder. And on it went.

It is shameful for radio stations to play songs that advocate mutilating and raping women. Government can't and shouldn't censor it, but decent advertisers could announce they will boycott any radio station that plays that kind of music. Within weeks these brutal, barbaric songs would be off the air.

Cultural signals are a powerful and legitimate means of enforcing proper behavior. One of the responsibilities of public leaders is to encourage the kind of public environment we want. Our culture should be sending over and over the message that young people should abstain from sexual intercourse until marriage, that work is a part of life, and that any male who does not take care of his children is a bum and deserves no respect. If you want a sense of the personal values we should be communicating to children, get the Boy Scout or Girl Scout handbook. Or go and look at *Reader's Digest* and *The Saturday Evening Post* from around 1955. Healthy societies send healthy signals to their children and to those who have become temporarily confused at any age. Look at the sick signals we are now sending through the entertainment industry and popular culture. Is it any wonder that society is so confused if not downright degenerate?

4. Emphasizing Family and Work

Charles Murray's *Losing Ground* was one of the first books to point out that the current welfare state is actually discouraging family formation, breaking up intact families, and trapping people in poverty for generations. Leon Dash's *When Children Want Children* then built a devastating case that the culture of poverty and violence was actually offering positive incentives for teenage girls to have children outside of marriage. Dash noted that over half the boys offered to marry the girl and were turned down. The tragedy is that the welfare state now offers young girls an alternative to marriage.

Yet while being pregnant outside of marriage may be appealing at first sight, it turns out to be a terrible trap. Three-fourths of all unmarried teen mothers end up on welfare within five years. More than 40 percent remain on the rolls for more than ten years. The daughters of teenage mothers are two and a half times more likely to become teen mothers themselves, and when they do, they are three times as likely to live in poverty.

Murray argues that the tax code, the welfare laws, and the rules of the bureaucracy all add up to a system that is antiwork, antifamily, and antiopportunity. We have to rewrite these laws so they do not punish people for taking responsibility. If a couple with children earns $11,000 apiece, they will pay $2,700 less in taxes if they remain unmarried. That's a 12 percent marriage tax. Then we wonder why births outside marriage have skyrocketed.

We have to reemphasize identifying the father and requiring the father to accept at least financial responsibility for the child (ideally he should also accept psychological and emotional responsibility, but let's start with the sense that if you have a child you have an obligation to help pay for that child's upbringing).

We need to revise welfare so that going to work never lowers your standard of living. When you add up housing, health care, food stamps, aid to family and dependent children, and other programs, there is actually a substantial disadvantage in joining the labor force. We need to redesign the system so people have a sense of reward at each step up the ladder of opportunity.

5. Tax Incentives for Work, Investment, and Entrepreneurship

People can work only when jobs are available; job creation requires investment. Today America's poorest neighborhoods offer such poor returns on investment that people simply won't go there to create jobs. The result is that few jobs are likely to be available, even if welfare rules are changed to encourage work. In addition, big cities often have the most red tape, the highest local taxes, and the most difficult bureaucracies. As a result, the poor are cheated out of jobs.

Hernando De Soto, a Peruvian economist, has written a brilliant book entitled *The Other Path*, in which he describes how lawyer-dominated big-city bureaucracies kill jobs in Latin America. Although he uses Lima, Peru, as his main example, every lesson applies to the United States.

In a brief introduction, Mario Vargas Llosa, a Peruvian novelist, describes the illegal activities of entrepreneurial Peruvians who refuse to let their government stop them from earning a living. At the time the book was written, 93 percent of the buses in Lima were illegal. The entire city had learned to operate outside the city's regulated transportation system.

Almost every public housing project in the United States has the same underground economy of people working for cash or barter without securing government licenses or paying taxes. Jack Kemp has been the leading advocate of "enterprise zones" that would encourage job creation within the legal system. Kemp has long proposed massive tax and regulatory breaks for anyone who would invest in poor neighborhoods. Since these neighborhoods pay almost no taxes anyway and since they drain the public treasury through welfare payments, the cost of giving them tax breaks would be relatively small. If new investment helped poor people make the long-term transition from welfare to productive work, these enterprise zones would more than pay for themselves. With Kemp's leadership, we are now working to apply this model in Washington, D.C. We hope to have a full-blown experiment by 1996.

People can create jobs as well as find jobs. Amway, Mary Kay, BeautiControl, Tupperware, and a host of other companies are examples of job creation. Anyone with a little money, some free time, and a willingness to learn marketing can make money. It is just as important to convince the poor that they can create their own jobs as it is to help them find jobs. We want to arouse an entrepreneurial spirit. A generation of small-business creation among African and Hispanic Americans would transform everything. If there were five Steve Jobses or one Bill Gates in Harlem, the entire nature of the community would change.

If city governments truly want to help the poor, they will make life dramatically easier for small businesses. What most poor neighborhoods need more than anything is a small-business renaissance. Cities should be cutting taxes and eliminating regulations to make it easy for poor people to start their own enterprises. Bill Marriott, founder of the famous hotel chain, started with a single pushcart. Today license regulations would probably make that pushcart illegal, and fees and taxes would make it unprofitable.

6. Reestablishing Savings and Property Ownership

If you are going to go to work or start your own small business, you have to believe you are going to keep the fruits of your labor. The history of immigrants in America has been a history of people working two and three jobs and scrimping and saving to put their children through school or open a first business. Immigrants dreamed of a better future and then worked to make those dreams come true. The greatest human damage done by the welfare state has been to kill people's dreams and destroy their ability to imagine themselves improving their lot.

The first step toward financial independence is to accumulate savings and acquire a little property. The current welfare system prohibits both. We want to ensure that, from day one, people who work hard can see their work pay off.

Part of this process involves giving people control over their own housing. Poor people ought to be given a chance to buy the property they live in. Public housing run as a cooperative or as a condominium would be vastly different from public housing run by middle-class bureaucrats who see the poor as clients rather than customers.

Jack Kemp has encouraged an experiment in the Kennilworth Apartments in Washington, D.C., in which residents took control of their own housing project. The first change they made was to require that maintenance people live in the project. Overnight the quality of maintenance improved. Custodians did a better job since, if they didn't, residents showed up at their door and complained. Trying to minimize their own work, maintenance workers quickly discovered who was breaking windows and engaging in vandalism. The guilty children were taken to their parents. The entire project began to look nicer within two months. When people are consumers instead of clients, their habits change drastically.

7. Learning as the Focus of Education

The greatest single misallocation of taxpayers' money has been the unionized monopolies of inner-city education. It is astonishing how much is spent per child on these cumbersome, red-tape-ridden bureaucracies—and how little ever gets to the individual child.

I was radicalized on this subject by former governor Tom Kean of New Jersey. He showed me a thousand-page study of the Jersey City schools, which were spending over $7,000 per child and hardly educating anyone. Governor Kean's study group discovered the schools had been looted by the local political machine for patronage purposes. There was a $54,000-a-year fire extinguisher inspector who failed to show up for three years. Not only was he freeloading, but the schools were left with faulty fire extinguishers. A fire would have been a disaster. The study led to a state takeover of the city school system.

My radicalization was completed by a *Chicago Tribune* series on one particularly bad school in the Windy City. After spending a year in the schools, a team of reporters wrote a devastating series of articles. The most telling was an interview with a teacher who was so destructive that every principal she had ever worked for had tried to fire her. The tenure system always saved her. She still had eleven years of teaching time left. When asked her professional goal, she said she wanted to retire with a full pension. This teacher regularly failed to educate thirty students a year, yet the system was designed to protect her incompetence. Remember, when young people fail to get educated in the Information Age, they lose all sense of purpose and dignity. When we tolerate a school that is failing to educate children, we put not just their education but their lives at risk.

The first breath of hope for me came in Milwaukee, where Polly Williams, a former welfare mother, has led a remarkable effort to reform the system. A Wisconsin state legislator and former state co-chair for Jesse Jackson's presidential campaign, Williams eventually concluded that inner-city children were being cheated by the education monopoly. She persuaded the legislature to adopt a voucher system that allows inner-city children to attend private schools at state expense. The Wisconsin teachers' union and the traditional liberals fought her bitterly, but Governor Tommy Thompson and the Republicans gave her the backing she needed. Even though the Republicans now control the state legislature, they have installed Williams as chair of the Inner City Education Reform Committee. She leads a broad bipartisan coalition that seeks to break the public-school monopoly and find new ways to educate poor children.

From home schooling to vouchers, from a drastic overhaul of the present system to allowing private companies to take over whole school districts—we simply have to take whatever steps are necessary to ensure that poor children can participate in the Information Age. There is no other strategy that will give them a full opportunity to pursue happiness.

8. Protection Against Violence and Drugs

Safety is simply the most fundamental concern of government. After all, none of our God-given rights matter much if we can be raped, mugged, robbed, or killed. And the poorest neighborhood is as entitled to be safe as the richest. No economic incentives a government can devise will entice businesses to open factories in a neighborhood where employees are likely to be in constant physical danger. Nor will any amount of education make up for your child being preyed upon by drug dealers and pimps. Addiction and prostitution will quickly wipe out the fruits of any educational reform.

In Part Four, I will outline proposals for ending the drug trade and saving children from violent crime. Here I will simply say that both measures are essential and should be applied first to the poorest neighborhoods. The United States Constitution was written to protect us from enemies both foreign and domestic. We are doing a good job on foreign enemies, but a pathetic job of protecting ourselves and our children from those who behave like domestic enemies.

Everything else will fail if we cannot suppress drugs and violent crime. Establishing safety is the first foundation of creating opportunity for the poor.

Summary

If we are truly serious about helping the poor, we must undertake all eight reforms simultaneously. The poor today are trapped both in a bureaucratic maze and in a culture of poverty and violence. No simple steps will suffice. It will take an immense effort and a lot of volunteers to replace the current welfare state with an opportunity society.

Imagine a poor child who is failing to learn in a public monopoly, whose life is at risk when she walks to the store, who knows no one who goes to work regularly, and who is likely to be pregnant at age twelve or thirteen. Now imagine that this child is your daughter. How hard would you work to save her life? How much effort would you put into forcing change? How intensely would you work to eliminate the bureaucracies that are exploiting her instead of serving her?

All I ask is that you look at your fellow Americans and decide that they deserve the same passion, the same commitment, the same courage you would show for your children. Together we can replace the culture of poverty and violence. Together we can replace the welfare bureaucracy. Together we can create a generation of hope and opportunity for all Americans.

CHAPTER 7

Balancing the Budget and Saving Social Security and Medicare

There are three essential reasons to balance the federal budget. First, it is morally the right thing to do. Second, it is financially the right thing to do. Third, each of us has a personal stake in it. In fact, your personal stake is probably a lot bigger than you realize.

Let me start with the morality of balancing the budget. Historically, it has always been self-evident in America that each generation had the obligation to live within its means. A major war was a legitimate excuse for massive borrowing. The Revolutionary War, the Civil War, and World Wars I and II were all financed in this way. But in peacetime, there has been a general rule that each generation would live within its means. As a result, our children would not be stuck with the task of paying off someone else's debt.

The principle was that we would pay off the mortgage and

leave the farm to our children. There was great delight in working hard and living within our means so that our children could be better off than we had been. Only in the last generation has this bias toward the future been reversed. Now we are borrowing against the farm to pay today's living expenses and leaving our children to pay off that debt.

Part of the problem comes from the psychology of the credit-card age. Both of my daughters went through what they called "credit-card hell." That was the period when they first had their own credit cards and learned painfully that they were actually expected to pay for the things they had charged.

In a sense, that is where we find ourselves as a country. John Boehner, one of our bright young leaders in Congress, made the point that the congressional voting card is the most expensive credit card in the world. Trillions of dollars in debt have been rung up on it. It has had seemingly unlimited credit. Each wave of politicians has taken care of its set of special interests without having to worry about fiscal limits. Since there was no requirement for a balanced budget, each member of the House or Senate or each Cabinet officer could always find room for one more item. No one had to be left totally unsatisfied. There were no limits and no hard priorities. Appeasing this year's interest groups was always more important than worrying about the burdens we were creating for our children and grandchildren.

In World War II this attitude of doing whatever it took was clearly right. The threat to freedom and American survival was sufficiently great that any amount of indebtedness was preferable to Nazi Germany and Imperial Japan dominating the world. During the Cold War there was some rationale for running a deficit. We were engaged in a struggle for the survival of freedom, and there was at least some justification for borrowing. The truth is, of course, that the cost of the military as a share of our economy declined for most of the Cold War and the great growth of government was in the domestic sector. We do not run a deficit because of defense spending. Our defense spending today is at the lowest share of the economy that it has been at since Pearl Harbor. We run a deficit because we have become a huge welfare state with massive transfer payments and a big centralized bureaucracy.

This rise of government has had a direct impact both on the burden that taxes now impose on our lives and on the fiscal burden of interest on the debt that is growing every year. Let's look first at the tax burden because the numbers are startling.

In 1900 the average household paid $1,370 in total government taxes (these are constant 1990 dollars). By 1950 that burden had grown to $6,970 per household. By 1994 the government burden of taxes had grown to $18,500 per household. While family incomes have grown in the interim, the growth in the tax percentage of median household income is almost as startling. In 1950 the median household paid 5 percent of its income in federal taxes. In 1970 it paid 16 percent of its income in federal taxes. By 1990 that figure had risen to 24 percent. If we could simply reduce the government to the size it was in 1970 (hardly a tiny government) we could return $4,000 a year to the average family budget. Imagine how much better off the average family would be if they could spend $4,000 more on their own children, their own education, their own savings. Are we really getting such efficient, effective government providing such vital services that it is better for the government to have the money than it is for the family that earned it?

Amazingly, this steady rise in taxes has still been too slow to keep up with government spending. The ability of the liberals to increase spending has outpaced anything Republicans could do in raising taxes. It is a little like having teenagers who are determined to spend 20 percent more than their allowances. If you give them ten dollars a week, they spend twelve. If you give them twenty dollars a week, they spend twenty-four. I watched the Reagan, Bush, and Clinton administrations talk themselves into tax increases to "fight the deficit," and each time the liberals simply took the new revenues as an excuse for even higher spending.

Despite the higher burden of taxation, the burden of federal indebtedness grows even higher. As I am writing this, we owe approximately $4.8 trillion in national debt. (Remember when a billion dollars was a lot? Now it's trillions and the billions hardly matter.) By the end of the decade, the Clinton administration expects us to owe approximately $6.5 trillion. By 2010 that debt will approach $8 trillion. When your national debt is more than doubling in fifteen peacetime years, there is something profoundly wrong with your budget and your finances.

This level of indebtedness has two immediate and profound impacts. First, the amount you have to pay in taxes just to pay off the *interest* on the debt keeps going higher and higher. Second, the government's need to borrow forces interest rates higher for all other borrowers—including industry, small businesses, families, home buyers, and state and local governments.

Let's look at the interest payments first. In 1995 we are paying $235 billion in taxes just to satisfy interest on the national debt. That money buys us no goods or services but is used only for the interest on money we have borrowed in previous years. Under the Clinton administration's current budget plan, interest on the debt will surpass the cost of national defense in 1997—$270 billion to $257 billion, respectively. That means you will pay more taxes to bondholders than you will pay to run the army, navy, air force, marine corps, intelligence agencies, and the defense bureaucracy. That level of deficit spending is clearly not sustainable for long.

But that's just the beginning. By the next century (now only five years away), the cost of servicing the accumulated debt—rising at $200 billion a year—will skyrocket. By 2005 we will be paying $412 billion in interest on the debt. Over the decade from 1995 to 2005 the cumulative interest will be more than $3.9 trillion. That's an amount almost equal to the current national debt. It is also two and a half times the current federal budget.

It is vital to remember that every penny paid to bondholders is a penny that can't go to education, health care, cleaning the environment, or leaving it in the family budget to allow you to decide how to spend it. It is also an extremely regressive form of income redistribution. The average bondholder has a considerably higher income than the average taxpayer. If we continue to allow money to be taken from middle-class taxpayers to pay wealthy bondholders, the inequity to the average American is going to be intolerable.

Besides squeezing taxpayers, the national debt puts an enormous additional burden on anyone else who wants to borrow money. This means anyone buying a home or a car, starting a small business, or simply putting clothes or household items on a credit card.

The United States government is the largest borrower in the world. All of its borrowing inevitably drives up interest rates and crowds out other borrowers. When the federal government is borrowing a billion dollars on every banking day (our rate of borrowing when the deficit is $250 billion) other borrowers have to take a place at the end of the line. Federal Reserve Chairman Alan Greenspan told me that a balanced budget would immediately bring down interest rates by a minimum of a 1.5 percent. A reasonable long-term estimate is 2 percent. Now, 2 percent may not seem like a lot, but when it's compounded every year you would be amazed at the difference it can bring.

If you buy a $75,000 house with a thirty-year mortgage, two extra points of interest cost you $1,248 a year, or $37,440 over the life of the mortgage. You might call it a "national deficit tax." If you pay for a $15,000 car over four years, you pay an extra $720 in national deficit tax. If you borrow $350,000 for six months to finance a small business or a family farm, you pay $3,000 in national deficit tax over just half a year.

Think of the burden every farm, every small business, every new factory and every family is now bearing simply to pay off the extra interest caused by the national deficit. A 1 percent drop in interest rates would save borrowers $300 billion over the next seven years.

All these numbers may seem remote and unimaginable, but for a child born this year the lifetime burden will be very real. If you have a child or a grandchild born in 1995, that child can expect to pay $187,000 in extra taxes over his or her lifetime just to pay the interest on the national debt. That comes to about $3,500 every year of the child's working life. Thus a child born this year faces an enormous burden in taxes *even before* paying for his or her own Social Security, Medicare, national defense, and education.

On the other hand, balancing the budget would create what might be considered a "balanced budget dividend." Estimates are that a 2 percent lower interest rate resulting from the prospect of a balanced federal budget would lead to six million more jobs over the next decade, a 16 percent increase in per capita income, $235 billion more revenue for the federal government, and $232 billion more for state and local governments—all without a tax increase. Lowering interest rates would also lower the interest that state and local governments pay for their own bond issues.

Thus, higher interest rates brought about by persistently running a national budget deficit creates a national deficit tax while lower interest rates brought about by persistently balancing the federal budget would lead to a balanced budget dividend. For a generation we have forgotten these kinds of financial realities.

While interest on the debt is a formidable national problem, it is dwarfed by the burden baby boomers will put on the system when they start retiring in 2010. That's only fifteen years from now. By 2013 the boomers will be drawing more out of Social Security than payroll taxes will be putting in. At that point the Social Security Trust Fund is supposed to go into operation.

However, there is one little-noticed catch to the Social Security Trust Fund. It is invested entirely in United States Treasury notes. In principle there is nothing wrong with holding

U.S. Treasury notes. They are among the safest investments in the world and bear a nice, reasonable rate of interest.

There are two possible scenarios. First, the Treasury can start paying off its debt to the Trust Fund with cash. That would be a considerable burden *even if* the federal budget were already in balance. Spending would have to be cut further or taxes raised to make up the difference. Second, the Treasury could go to the private market and borrow more money.

The problem with the second approach is that the U.S. government is already hiding a good bit of its borrowing by selling $50 to $100 billion in notes a year to the Social Security system. Once the Trust Fund's surplus runs out, this money will no longer be available for financing the federal deficit. In fact, the situation will be reversed. The Treasury will have to borrow both to make up the current accounts and to pay off all its Social Security borrowings from previous years. By 2025, the Treasury could end up borrowing *$2.5 trillion each year*—ten times the current figure—to meet its obligations.

It is obvious that the world financial system could not provide this kind of money. In that case, there could only be one possible outcome—hyperinflation. The government would simply print money as a way of renouncing its accumulated obligations. Among other things, borrowers from previous years would be paid off in money that was worth much, much less. It wouldn't be the first time it has happened.

The Founding Fathers were all men of property who believed in honest money. They had watched states like Rhode Island begin to print their own paper money in order to erase their Revolutionary War debts and decided the country needed a strong central government with a sound currency. They all had studied history and knew that many popular governments in the ancient world had destroyed themselves by debasing their currency and cheating their citizens of savings. The Founding Fathers assumed that the value of money was based on gold. As a result, they wrote into the Constitution a provision making it illegal for the states to coin money or "make any Thing but gold and silver Coin a Tender in Payment of Debts."

Money is both a medium of exchange and a standard of value. When the government gives you a dollar it is implicitly promising that this dollar will be worth the same amount when you cash it in. Jack Kemp likes to note that the value of money was so stable in the nineteenth century that his grandfather once bought a one-hundred-year railroad bond that paid 1 percent interest a year. It was assumed that the gold-backed dollar would be worth the same amount one hundred years later. Today it is normal to expect a compounded 4 to 6 percent annual devaluation of the dollar over ten years.

The destructive powers of hyperinflation were driven home to me by Ted Hirsch, the mayor of Carollton, Georgia. When I was first elected to Congress, Mayor Hirsch, a strong supporter and a neighbor, came by to show me a set of bills he had from Weimar Germany. A Jew born in Germany, who had fled just before Hitler's takeover, Ted knew from bitter experience that inflation played a huge role in destroying the Weimar Republic. Nothing can lead to dictatorship faster, he said, than when the middle class loses its savings through hyperinflation. The Weimar notes he showed me ran from one hundred marks at the beginning to an overprinted bill stamped "one billion marks." In the last days of the Weimar inflation, it was not uncommon for people to bring wheelbarrows of money just to pay for groceries.

Throughout history, governments and politicians have turned in desperation to inflation as a way of paying the costs of their spending and borrowing. Inflation often starts painlessly. For a while a majority can even benefit because there are more borrowers than lenders. But then people start to anticipate inflation and a casino atmosphere takes over. "Gambling replaces commerce," as Andrew Dickson White, a historian of the French Revolution's inflationary period, once put it. Under President Carter we reached 11 percent inflation and 19 percent interest rates—almost four times the normal peacetime rate from the previous two centuries. People were buying gold, antiques, baseball cards—anything to get out of holding their own country's money. Savings were devalued, and plans for the future became totally unpredictable. Only when Ronald Reagan took the helm was inflation brought under control again.

Daniel Yankelovich describes this need for a secure relationship between people and their government as a "giving and getting contract." People want to know what they have to give during their lifetime and what they will get back for having done their duty. In a stable, healthy society, there is a strong sense that if you work hard, save your money, pay your taxes, and fulfill the duties of citizenship, then the government will keep things stable enough for you to collect your rewards. Inflation strikes at the very heart of this "giving and getting contract." It says that those who borrow, gamble, and spend today do better than those who work hard and live frugally. Hyperinflation absolutely destroys any sense of trust and stability between people and their government.

Baby boomers need to realize that the federal government must balance its operating budget if they are ever going to be able to collect their Social Security. Now is the time to put our house in order. Every time you see an insurance company or an investment company urging you to plan for your retirement, you ought to apply the same logic to the whole country. If individuals and families must plan years ahead for retirement, isn't the same thing true of generations and nations?

Those who think the situation is still too distant to worry about need look no further than Medicare to understand that America is on the precipice of substantial fiscal problems. Medicare is the foundation of health care for our senior citizens. It is a government monopoly and therefore inefficient, wasteful, and slow to adapt to innovations in technology and management. As a result, the system is rapidly growing out of control. Fraud, waste, and mismanagement divert resources that ought to go to the medical care of our senior citizens.

Under the current projections of the Medicare board of trustees, Medicare will spend $2 billion more than it receives in 1996, $39 billion more in 2002, and $71 billion more in 2005. Outlays are projected to rise from $200 billion at the end of the century to $600 billion by 2014. Costs are currently doubling every seven years. Such a rate of increase is clearly unsustainable. It will either bankrupt Medicare or bankrupt America.

At this rate, maintaining the Medicare Trust Fund would require raising Medicare taxes 125 percent and senior citizens' annual premiums 300 percent by 2002. Even that will only buy time. If growth continues, taxes and premiums will have to be raised again and again. Sooner or later taxpayers or senior citizens or both will rebel.

If we are going to save our senior citizens' health system, our baby boomers' retirement, and our children's future we are going to have to remake the federal government and balance the budget. As I noted earlier, this is a moral necessity, a financial necessity, and a personal obligation for all Americans. Our personal future will be determined by whether or not we have the courage to undertake the task.

Actually, balancing the budget is a pretty straightforward process. Once we set our minds to the task, it should not be all that difficult. In 1995 the federal government took in revenues of $1.4 trillion. By 2002 the government should have revenues of $1.8 trillion. *Slowing* the growth of government spending so that seven years from now we are spending only $1.8 trillion would produce a balanced budget.

One way to think about the scale of the challenge is to look at the last seven years. From 1989 through 1995 the federal government has spent $9.5 trillion. During the next seven years a balanced budget would allow us to spend $11.7 trillion. In other words, we could spend $2.2 trillion *more* over the next seven years and still balance the budget. It's just a matter of cutting out the extra increases.

I have argued consistently that Social Security must be off

the table in any discussion of a balanced budget. Social Security is the most widely accepted government contract in America. It is also the single most popular government program. Furthermore, the current generation of politicians has not earned the necessary trust to talk about retirement programs. There is plenty of government left to remake even if we protect Social Security.

The hysteria that liberals were able to raise over the school lunch program proposal (which slows the growth in its spending from a 5.2 percent annual increase to a 4.6 percent annual increase) indicates that no one can realistically hope to balance the budget by tampering with Social Security. Can you imagine the scare campaign that liberals would launch if anyone tried to balance the budget using Social Security funds? On the other hand, if we can balance the budget we will have earned the trust of the baby boomers and their children. At that point, I believe, we can open a dialogue about creating a safer retirement for future generations.

If Social Security is off the table, that takes $2.3 trillion out of consideration. That allows us to spend $8.8 trillion on non–Social Security functions. That is a $1.3 trillion increase over the past seven years—and a 17 percent increase over the next seven years.

It tells you how much money liberals need to run their programs when a 17 percent increase in non–Social Security spending over seven years is seen by Washington as a terrible *cut* in spending. In 1974 the liberals passed an accounting gimmick that provided automatic increases in spending each year. This is called the "current services budget." Any increase that is *less* than the programmed increase is called a "cut." Thus, liberals claim regularly that they are "cutting" spending when they increase spending less than the amount prescribed by the "current services" automatic pilot.

Imagine your child had a ten-dollar allowance and you decided to increase it by two dollars a week. You announce a twelve-dollar-a-week allowance, thinking your child will be grateful. Instead, using the liberals' "current services" logic, your child announces that he or she was automatically due an increase to twelve dollars and fifty cents, and you have "cut" his or her allowance. Sounds nutty, doesn't it? Note that it also builds a huge bias in favor of constant increases in spending.

It is this gimmick that has allowed liberals to scream that Republicans were "cutting" the school lunch program ("taking food out of the mouths of children," as President Clinton so politely put it) when we were actually providing a 4.5 percent annual increase over the next five years. The liberals' "current services" budget had already called for larger increases. Therefore, our increase was supposed to be a "cut." If you are a taxpayer, the liberals have rigged the system against you in favor of ever-escalating spending. Even a big increase is only holding back from what they have already planned.

Governor John Sununu was the first person to drive home for me the craziness of this upward spiral of spending. When Governor Sununu came to Washington in January 1989 to become President Bush's chief of staff, he had just been governor of the most frugal state in the country. New Hampshire's motto is "Live Free or Die!" and the citizens of the Granite State live that way. They are deeply opposed to tax increases and still rely on annual town meetings to adopt annual budgets. Governor Sununu understood instantly that the liberals had built a system that gave them tremendous upward leverage in the budget debate. In 1989 he persuaded the Bush administration to send to Congress a budget based on the previous year's spending rather than on automatic upward increases. However, in subsequent years the Bush administration gave in and adopted the "current services" method. (Jimmy Carter's "zero-based budgeting" was another forlorn attempt to deal with this problem!)

When House Republicans took over on January 4, 1995, one of the first rules we adopted was to outlaw "current services" baseline budgeting for House purposes. We are fighting very aggressively to return the federal budget to the same standard used by every state, city, county, corporation, and family in America. No one else gets to make up a wish-list number and then proclaim that anything short of that is a cut. Wouldn't you love to negotiate your salary or review your family finances with those ground rules? And wouldn't you go broke trying to operate that way?

We are convinced that with very diligent, hard work we can achieve a balanced budget by 2002. This will mean setting priorities. It will require us to remake parts of the federal government. It will involve cutting out waste and unnecessary bureaucracy. It will require replacing the welfare state with an opportunity society. It will require new approaches to education and health care.

We believe the American people are ready for an adult effort to balance the budget and remake the federal government. We are convinced the American people are mature enough to engage in a genuine dialogue about their future, their children's future, and their country's future. We also believe the American people can tell when someone is sincerely trying to do the right thing for the country.

Remember, balancing the federal budget by itself will probably take seven years of unrelenting effort. Then, having balanced the federal budget, we need to establish a sinking fund to pay down the national debt. Bringing the national debt (which by then will be about $6.5 trillion) down to an acceptable size will take about two generations of setting firm priorities within a frugal environment.

Nevertheless, we are ready to go to work. Balancing the federal budget is the right thing to do for America.

CHAPTER 8

Decentralizing Power

We may well be nearing the end of the century of big government. It is hard for those who grew up with today's bureaucratic, centralized systems to realize that only a century ago our current scale of government would have been rejected as unimaginable by both Britain and America. During the Victorian and Edwardian eras people expected dramatically more self-reliance and local initiative and control than anything we have today.

In a sense, the modern infatuation with big government can be traced to the last two years of World War I and to Ludendorff's control of the German economy. Lenin and Mussolini were both inspired by the centralized planning and control of the wartime German empire. Politicians and intellectuals everywhere were attracted to the idea that their power and intelligence could put them in control of other people's lives and wealth, which could then be used to great purposes.

War and national crises have long been the two best breeders of big government. The Great Depression under both Hoover and FDR left us with a centralized bureaucracy dominated by Washington.

World War II was the ultimate creator of the large state in America. The success of our temporary effort to mobilize an entire free people (something we actually did better than the Germans) intoxicated a number of liberal intellectuals. There is a direct correlation between John Kenneth Galbraith's experience manipulating wage and price controls as a young man in Washington and his lifelong enthusiasm for government planning. Many young people who were at the center of the war effort could never distinguish between the temporary subordination of a free people to a great national cause and the inevitable decay and dishonesty that would come if wartime controls were transmuted into a permanent peacetime system.

The Cold War gave big government a good excuse to hang on for yet another generation. The presumption that bureaucracy could accomplish great things lasted a long time. Gradually, however, with leadership from Goldwater and Reagan in the political world and Bill Buckley's *National Review* and the *Wall Street Journal*'s editorial page on the intellectual front, the case against the centralized state began to make headway.

With Reagan's victory in the 1980s, antibureaucratic economists such as Nobel Prize winners Friedrich von Hayek and Milton Friedman began to win attention as guides to practical thought. The argument between freedom and state power began to be heard as it had not been since the beginning of World War I.

With the end of the Cold War, the case for a strong central government has been dramatically weakened. The time has come for a reversion to first principles. In America, one of those first principles is that power resides first and foremost with the individual citizen. In America, individual citizens earn their bread, and the government had better have an overwhelming reason for taking it away from them. In America, the independent citizen is the foundation on which the whole society rests.

It is fascinating to go back to the Founding Fathers and read about the Whiskey Rebellion against the tax on corn liquor in the early 1790s. Here was President Washington, father of the country, winner of the Revolutionary War, first President of the new Republic, and here was a group of cantankerous, bullheaded farmers from west of the Alleghenies, ready to fight rather than have the distant government tax their primary method of commerce—turning corn into corn liquor. Ultimately, cooler heads prevailed. But the sentiment for questioning the national capital had been established and has never left us.

Seen in this light, the recent movie *The Last of the Mohicans* is a quintessentially American film. The central figure is a woodsman who is used to being on his own and intends to remain independent no matter what the cost. A British officer, coming from an orderly and aristocratic society, cannot imagine the independence of mind and spirit at the heart of America. At one point, the American says he is going to "Caintukeee" and the British officer asks in bewilderment how he can leave the ordered and regulated military society. "Face north, turn left, and walk five hundred miles," the frontiersman responds. That scene says everything about the difference between the two societies.

In our day, too many intellectuals, columnists, and bureaucrats have come to accept the European notion that government matters more than its citizens. Washington is filled with presumptions about the importance of central government. People there talk and act as if the federal bureaucracy were the be-all and end-all of American life.

Yet the story of America has been that freedom starts by maximizing local initiative and local resources. De Tocqueville's description of voluntary organizations as the backbone of America would remain true today if these efforts were not completely overshadowed by a gigantic federal bureaucracy. For Ben Franklin, solving public problems meant starting volunteer fire departments, volunteer philosophical societies, and volunteer libraries. Franklin was postmaster general for the colonies and knew there were things that had to be done at a national level.

But generally he turned neither to national government nor to state and local government but to organized volunteers to get things done.

The last part of the nineteenth century and the years before World War I were the golden age of volunteerism. Andrew Carnegie built over 2,500 libraries throughout the world and helped found the first pension fund for college professors, the Teacher's Insurance and Annuities Association (TIAA). The Boy Scouts, the Girl Scouts, the New York Zoological Society, the Young Men's Christian Association, the American Museum of Natural History, the Salvation Army—all of these and hundreds more were formed in an explosion of volunteerism and charity. People turned first not to government but to themselves and their neighbors when they sought to solve problems.

The nineteenth-century respect for the public's money was driven home to me by the memoirs of one of General Ulysses S. Grant's assistants. Immediately after accepting Lee's surrender, General Grant boarded a train for Washington. En route, on the very afternoon the war had ended, he began to draft orders to demobilize the army so that the maximum amount of money could be saved for the American people. Contrast this frugality with the modern federal bureaucracies' end-of-the-year binges in which they race to spend the remainder of the annual appropriation so that no money will have to be given back to the Treasury.

It is against this backdrop that our effort to decentralize and devolve government power should be viewed. We are not simply trying to move a few offices out of Washington while retaining the heart of the twentieth-century behemoth. We are trying to reestablish the American value of individual liberty and the citizens' first claim to their own money. What we have done so far is only a small step in the right direction.

The last sixty years has seen so much centralization in Washington that at this point the best we can do is to start by shifting power back to the state capitals. Power in fifty different cities is better than power centralized in one city.

Yet our ultimate goal is to move power even beyond the state capitals. Many mayors and county commissioners are deeply suspicious of state governments and would prefer bloc grants and programs that come straight to them. In their minds, local government is the best government, and they stand ready to accept power and money if Washington will only give it to them.

However, much as I sympathize with both state and local governments, what we really want to do is to devolve power all the way out of government and back to working American families. We want to leave choices and resources in the hands of individuals and let them decide if they prefer government, the profit-making sector, the nonprofit sector, or even no solution at all to their problems. It is important to remember that freedom ultimately includes the right to say no. If you must say yes to something—or everything—then you are not free.

Dealing with a free people is often difficult and frustrating. As Dick Armey says, "Democracy is a damned inconsiderate system." Other people have their own ideas and prejudices about your view. It is hard to lead a free people; in many ways it is much easier to get the job done by simply allowing a bureaucracy to tell people what to do. Yet in the long run, the strength of a free society is the commitment of every person to solve real problems and bear real responsibilities. If we take away the freedom to make mistakes, then we take away the freedom to grow and learn. If we refuse to grant this freedom, we drain a free society of its human strength.

The liberal model is that an enlightened national capital will establish the correct laws and hire the bureaucrats to enforce them. This was the orderly world of Robert McNamara that was destroyed by North Vietnamese stubbornness. It is the identical theory that is behind every centralized bureaucracy of the Great Society.

Instead, Republicans envision a decentralized America in which responsibility is returned to the individual. We believe in volunteerism and local leadership. We believe that a country with ten million local volunteer leaders is stronger than one with a thousand brilliant national leaders.

Our model puts a premium on diversity, creativity, and the ability of free people to invent different ways of solving problems. We prefer to talk about goals, but processes count just as much. We think a free people can demonstrate amazing ingenuity if given a chance.

The centralized bureaucratic model inherently distrusts organized local people and local governments and believes that a Washington-based system must issue detailed prescriptions or local people will invariably do the wrong thing.

There was certainly some justification for a centralized bureaucratic effort when one-third of the nation was legally segregated. The federal government had to be prepared to intervene to protect minorities from the legal oppression of state and local governments. In 1965 there was perhaps a good case for centralized supervision during an era of change.

Today, however, as long as the federal government enforces the basic civil and voting rights (and I approve using the full power of the federal government on both of these issues), it is unnecessary to have a Washington bureaucracy overseeing the actions of honestly elected local officials.

In Atlanta, Georgia, there is now an African-American mayor, Bill Campbell, and an African-American majority on the city council. It seems a little strange to have white bureaucrats in Washington, D.C., deciding whether elected black Atlantans care about poor black Atlantans. By what right does a Washington bureaucrat have to stand in judgment of Mayor Campbell? What theory assumes that if you work in a federal office building you are morally superior to a local government official?

Our desire to devolve power out of Washington and disperse it to local governments is reinforced by everything we are learning about the Information Age. Virtually every effort to create more competitive companies has involved returning authority to the person closest to the problem. From the military to commercial work, experts have found over and over again that the flatter the organization chart and the more decentralized the decision making, the more authority that can be given to the person who is most informed about the probable outcome. All of these trends validate our effort to shift power out of Washington.

The quality of the new generation of governors, mayors, county commissioners, and state legislators encourages us to believe that America is ready for more decentralized government. Governors Tommy Thompson of Wisconsin, John Engler of Michigan, William Weld of Massachusetts, Christie Todd Whitman of New Jersey, Mayors Brett Schundler of Jersey City, Richard Riordan of Los Angeles, Ed Rendell of Philadelphia, Rudy Giuliani of New York, John Norquist of Milwaukee, Michael White of Cleveland, Victor Ashe of Knoxville, and Steve Goldsmith of Indianapolis—together they are a new generation of leadership that is hungering for responsibility. When I attend meetings of the American Legislative Exchange Council, I am stunned by the quality, educational level, and energy of new state legislators. It is clear that the Information Age, the rise of C-SPAN, the development of computer bulletin boards, and the development of new legislative associations are all accelerating the learning curve of this next generation of leaders.

The Information Age will actually make it easier for these positive changes to be transferred to other systems. A model that is working in one place can rapidly be adopted by others. That is why we believe turning welfare back to the fifty states will increase the likelihood of real breakthroughs in our ability to help people. Once one state or city makes a breakthrough the ideas will be shared and rapidly imitated in others. Computer conferences, faxes, teleconferences, and special meetings will move ideas much more quickly than the old way of shuffling papers from one wing of the bureaucracy to another. People at the local level are motivated about solving their own problems in a way no distant bureaucrat can be. It is this combination of decentralized authority and rapidly improving national information systems that makes us so confident that dispersion of federal authority will prove to be vastly superior to the bureaucratic model in which we are currently languishing.

This drive to decentralize should not be mistaken as a plea for weak government. I strongly favor the Constitution over the Articles of Confederation. The Constitution is a device for strong central government, and so it should remain. Keeping our money honest, regulating our trade in the world market, maintaining our national defense, breaking the back of illegal drugs, sustaining a nationwide database on convicted felons and the mentally ill so that we sell guns only to honest and law-abiding citizens, sustaining a nationwide system of retirement, investing in research and development at the level of basic knowledge so we can continue to advance (as we did as early as the Lewis and Clark Expedition)—all of these are but a few of the legitimate duties of the federal government.

The current federal budget is over $1.5 trillion. A reasonable federal government would probably spend $1 trillion. Even liberals should find solace in this solution. Government would be leaner but more focused, more effective at its designated responsibilities. Beyond that, as the Tenth Amendment states: "The powers not delegated to the United States by the Constitution, nor prohibited by it to the States, are reserved to the States respectively, or to the people."

PART THREE

The Contract
with America

CHAPTER 9

The Contract
with America and the
Campaign of 1994

The Contract with America helped focus the 1994 campaign, unified the House Republican Party, and provided a dynamic direction for the first Republican Congress in forty years. Eventually, historians and political scientists will study it as a unique instrument in American politics—there is no comparable congressional document in our two-hundred-year history.

The Contract actually had a fairly long lineage. During the 1980 campaign, Republican National Chairman Bill Brock introduced me to Charlie McWhorter, a vice president of AT&T and cofounder of the Newport Jazz Festival, who had a reputation as a great innovator in Republican politics. Charlie suggested that all Republican federal candidates should gather on the Capitol steps and pledge a common platform. It would prove how serious we were about reform and point up a sharp contrast with the malaise of the Carter years. I loved the idea, and the Senate and Reagan campaigns signed on.

In early October, the entire Republican ticket assembled, calling for the Kemp-Roth tax cuts, a strengthened national defense, and significant cuts in federal spending. David Broder, one of the country's leading political journalists, wrote a favorable column about it. A number of our senate and congressional candidates profited. We picked up thirty-three seats in the House and won a majority in the Senate after several very close races. Without the event at the Capitol we might not have won the Senate.

While the 1980 event seemed worth repeating, circumstances did not lend themselves for the next six elections. Either the political environment was wrong or the platform was not universally popular or the leading candidates did not want to risk tying themselves to the party. There was always some reason.

By 1993, however, the world had changed considerably. A young, energetic generation of conservative leaders had come of age. Meanwhile, President Clinton's popularity was stuck in the mid-40s—close to the plurality by which he won the 1992 election. His advocacy of unpopular social issues had alienated much of middle America. Tax increases had angered the small-business community. His health plan had collapsed and his much heralded welfare reform had never materialized. Support for term limits was growing at a fantastic pace. Various congressional scandals had made it clear that after forty years of power, the Democratic party was worn out.

The first indication we had that the political environment was changing was the outpouring of eager and attractive congressional candidates during the fall of 1993. Our weaknesses at the federal level had often been mirrored at the state level. Democrats controlled thirty governorships and thirty-one state legislatures, while Republicans had eighteen governors and complete control of only seven legislatures. Even such bastions of conservatism as Montana, Nevada, and Oklahoma were controlled by Democrats. Parts of the South had not elected Republican majorities since the Civil War. (I was the only Republican in Georgia's congressional delegation for six of my eight terms in office.) We had had no farm team to help us play in the big leagues. For decades, scores of Democratic seats around the country had gone uncontested. This long incumbency discouraged many people from even trying. But in October 1993, while heading our campaign effort, Bill Paxon, a congressman from upstate New York, and Congressman Jim Nussle of Iowa reported that they were having fantastic success in recruiting new faces. They were mostly young, educated people with professional backgrounds—many very religious—who had grown up questioning the legacy of the 1960s and were critical of liberalism both on economic and social grounds.

All of this fell into place in two special elections in May 1994. The first was for an Oklahoma seat being vacated by Glenn English, a member of the Watergate class of 1974, who was stepping down to become chief lobbyist for the Rural Electric Cooperative Association. Frank Lucas, a three-term member of the Oklahoma house, was our candidate, running against Dan Webber, press secretary for Senator David Boren. Oklahoma had a long Democratic tradition, but early polls showed us that dissatisfaction with the Clinton health plan and other social issues had put our candidate in the lead. On May 10 Lucas won 56–44, a surprisingly easy victory. It was the first real sign that something big was happening among the electorate.

Only two weeks later, we faced a special election in Kentucky for a seat that had not been held by a Republican since 1865. No one gave us a serious chance. The unexpected, easy victory in Oklahoma, however, inspired us to put all of our efforts into the campaign.

Our candidate, Ron Lewis, had never held public office. He ran a small Christian bookstore, which immediately led Democrats to paint him as a fanatic of the "religious right." Unfortunately, while this tactic looked great in Washington it didn't play well in Kentucky. People in Ron's district were deeply disturbed by the decay in Washington and thought a congressman with moral values might be a good thing. Although we had focused exclusively on Oklahoma until just two weeks before the Kentucky election, we now shifted money and resources into the new race. With only thirteen days to go, our candidate had very limited name recognition and lagged far behind in the polls.

Fortunately, his opponent, Joe Prather, had voted for tax increases a number of times while serving as Kentucky senate majority leader. The campaign committee developed an ad in which a picture of the Democratic nominee's face gradually morphed into President Clinton's and then back again. The voice-over reminded people of the President's 1993 tax increase, the largest in the nation's history. The ad was a fantastic success and drew thousands of votes our way.

On May 24, the results were more than we could ever have expected. Ron Lewis won a smashing 55–45 victory. (He won again, 60–40, in November.) Suddenly, activists and donors started taking our prospects seriously for the coming election. The Democrats also sagged a bit. The national health plan lost momentum and never recovered the sense of inevitability it had possessed only a few months before. A number of Democrats viewed the Oklahoma and Kentucky results as bad omens, and began drawing away from the Clinton administration.

As it turned out Ron Lewis became a pathbreaker, both in his unprecedented victory and in the way he entered the House. When new members are sworn in, they customarily give a brief speech. Normally this is a thank-you to supporters and a promise to work hard as a representative. In the middle of his speech, however, Lewis suddenly said, "Excuse me, Mr. Speaker, there is something I must do right now." He strode over to the House Clerk and signed the discharge petition to release the A-to-Z Spending Cuts Bill from the committee where the Democrats had bottled it up. House Republicans went wild with applause at this stunning break in tradition.

As the fall campaign began to build momentum, our greatest concern was that the politics would turn too negative. We knew the Democrats were in trouble and figured their strategy would be to run a scorched-earth campaign. Perot voters were one of the keys to our campaign. We knew they were mad at Congress, but knew they were also generally mad at politicians and were likely to be turned off by a negative campaign. If the mudslinging got bad they would probably stay home, significantly cutting into our chances of victory.

At the same time, we realized that our greatest mistake would be to win control of the House and the Senate and not have a clear blueprint for the future. Our fear was that seventy-five eager freshmen would arrive in Washington, walk around in dazed happiness for a few months, and then slowly be taken into the fold by lobbyists, media personalities, and the rest of the Washington establishment. That would have been worse than losing the election.

Our new congressional leaders—Dick Armey and Tom DeLay of Texas, John Boehner and John Kasich of Ohio, Robert Walker of Pennsylvania, and Bill Paxon of New York—were all deeply committed to a genuine revolution. We did not want big offices or fancy perks. We were citizens with conviction, values, and a vision of a better America. We wanted to set out a plan and then shock everyone by actually implementing it.

In January 1994 the House Republican conference had taken about half its members to a weekend retreat in Salisbury, Maryland. We had a delightful weekend of brainstorming. Frank Luntz, a bright young pollster, argued that we had to stake out a strong case for reform if we wanted to get the country's attention. The members developed the "Salisbury Statement," which became the first draft of the Contract.

Revolutions have to be built one step at a time. The first step was to commit the party to the idea that we should run on idealistic bold reforms and be prepared to keep our word. By June we had agreed to hold a Capitol steps event in September involving ten major program statements. The ten points basically selected themselves as deeply felt desires of the American people. We knew from long experience that people were desperate for a law requiring Congress to obey the same laws as everyone else. We knew that there was overwhelming support for the balanced budget amendment, the line-item veto, and term limits. As the party of small businesses and family farms we knew that litigation reform and regulatory reform were strongly supported. As conservatives and advocates of a prowork and profamily America we knew that welfare reform, a child tax credit, increased savings opportunities, and capital gains tax cuts to increase economic growth would strengthen America. Finally, as conservatives we felt the liberals had weakened our national defense and our laws against criminals and child pornographers. We believed that these should be strengthened. It can literally be said that the Contract with America grew out of our conversations with the American people and out of our basic conservative values.

Dick Armey then appointed ten task forces so that each item in the Contract would have its own working group. Bill Paxon made sure every candidate in the country had the chance to review the material and submit suggestions. John Boehner and his top staff member, Barry Jackson, worked out the staging of the actual event. At the suggestion of Pete DuPont, former governor of Delaware, we created contracts at the state, county, and local levels as well.

On September 14 I took a four-day swing through the country for our House candidates. On board, working out the fall and winter schedules, were Dan Meyer, my chief of staff; Joe Gaylord, my political chief of staff; and Steve Hanser, my general adviser. As the airplane climbed out of National Airport, I asked casually, "Are we planning for speaker or minority leader?"

Gaylord, probably the best student of congressional campaigns in the country, shot back, "You'd better plan to be speaker because that's the way it's going to be." We all stared at him in shock. All of us had probably thought privately that we might soon be in the majority, but here was our congressional expert telling us it was a sure thing. The certainty in Joe's voice had stopped us in our tracks.

From then on we adopted a ritual for every trip. Joe would go through the entire country from Maine to Hawaii telling us what he thought would happen in all 435 congressional races. His grasp of details was astonishing. Right off, his lowest estimate was that we would pick up thirty-five seats. That would put us above our previous high since 1956 of 192 seats and, with the help of a handful of conservative Democrats, give us a working majority. His best estimate was that we would net forty-five to fifty-three seats, enough for a clear majority. (We eventually netted fifty-two.) Barring a major Democratic breakthrough or Republican blunder, we were going to be the new majority. You can imagine the growing sense of excitement on those plane rides.

Frankly, we expected the White House to ignore the September event. Lee Atwater had taught me this lesson in 1990. At that point, Democratic Senate Majority Leader George Mitchell and House Speaker Tom Foley were getting a lot of attention in Washington for attacking President George Bush. The Republican leadership urged a counterattack. "Do any of you know what Mitchell's national recognition figures are?" Atwater finally asked. None of us had any idea. "It's thirty percent," he said. "The President's is ninety-seven percent. Why should we raise the recognition level for two virtual unknowns?" Although Lee was no longer with us, I thought of him many times during the 1994 campaign.

The Friday before the event, however, Tony Blankley, my press secretary, received a surprise phone call from a White House reporter. The President was about to launch a full-scale attack on the Contract. What was our reaction? Frankly, we were overjoyed. The White House response ensured that the Contract would be the subject of the weekend talk shows. Coverage was certain to skyrocket. The White House counterattack had turned a potential inside-page photo opportunity into the centerpiece of the campaign.

One reason we were confident is that we had done our homework. The first item in the Contract—applying all the laws of the nation to Congress itself—was viewed favorably by 90 percent of the American people. The balanced budget amendment, the line-item veto, welfare reform, term limits, the $500 tax credit for children, and an enforceable death penalty all had 80 percent support. The least recognized items—regulatory reform and litigation reform—still had 60 percent support. Which one of these items was President Clinton going to attack?

Our conclusion was that the Democrats' reflexive opposition to the Contract was another example of how ideologically opposed they were to any change in the status quo and how far out of touch they had become with the American people.

When we finally stood on the Capitol steps on September 27, we had thoroughly briefed our candidates. Everyone knew the details and was prepared to defend the issues against Democratic criticisms. The day was windy but beautiful. Barry Jackson, the director of the event, had strung a magnificent banner across the Capitol steps. The event got substantial press coverage and we were on our way.

The Washington press corps immediately got it into their heads that the Contract was a big mistake. Reporter after reporter, columnist after columnist, declared that we had blown our chances just as it appeared we might win a majority. Editorial writers attacked us for supporting welfare reform, the death penalty, a balanced budget, a line-item veto, and term limits. Some liberal columnists even said that we were pandering to the American people—precisely because the vast majority agreed with us! In their lexicon, only elite opinions count.

For our part the Contract brought our campaign completely into focus. The sense that victory was within our grasp made a big difference in the campaign. For decades Republicans had entered the congressional races with the sense that, ultimately, we were going to remain in the minority. This became a self-fulfilling prophecy. It is harder to raise money when major donors know the Democrats are going to win. It is harder to recruit candidates and get the media's attention. It took unusual courage for leaders like Bob Michel to sustain a minority party for so long, but minority status had ultimately become debilitating. By October most of our people were convinced we could win. It gave us a heady boost in morale and resources.

In the final weeks, Bob Dole and I campaigned together around the country. Dole was tireless and willing to travel everywhere. He may have been partly motivated by presidential ambitions but, as a seasoned professional, he knew things were breaking for our whole party. Everywhere we went the crowds were enthusiastic. The sense of unity gave us a campaign that was almost unprecedented for Republicans in this century.

Right to the end, the press continued to speculate that some last-minute surge or stroke of luck would continue the old order. There was a wave of "Democrats-make-a-comeback" stories. But in the end, even the reporters seemed to sense that something out of the ordinary was happening.

Marianne and I spent election night in Georgia with our family and friends. We set up a national information command post in the Cobb Galleria Convention Center, a wonderful new facility that was perfect for the developing crowds and media coverage. The networks and major newspapers had all sent reporters. My mom and dad and my two daughters and their husbands joined us, along with lots of relatives and friends. People who had spent years supporting House Republicans during long seasons of being in the minority were thrilled to be part of "the big evening." Guy Vander Jagt, my friend and mentor, came down with his wife, Carol, to see his life's dream of a Republican House majority come true.

As the evening wore on, it became clear that history was going to be made. We had won a decisive victory in my home district with 64 percent of my constituents voting for me, the biggest margin of my career. As the night wore on, I spoke on live television interviews broadcast all over the country. The convention center was full of Republicans getting more excited by the minute. Congressman Mac Collins had won a tough campaign in the district that contained a portion of my old district on the south side of Atlanta. Late in the evening he came up to join us. We were exhausted and exhilarated. At two-thirty in the morning, I sat around with about forty of our strongest supporters and started to discuss the scale of our victory. We had gained twelve governorships, eight Senate seats, and fifty-two House seats without a single incumbent losing anywhere. What advice did they have in these first hours of our new majority status?

We got into an interesting discussion about the word "growth." In several interviews I had already said that being speaker would be a much bigger responsibility than being minority whip. I hoped to learn and grow in the job. I would have thought these words were positive, but several of my conservative supporters joined my friend John Uhlman to reject the phrasing. In their view "growth" is what the Washington press corps likes to say about someone who comes to Washington and betrays grassroots people. "We don't want you to grow in the eyes of the Washington news media," they said. "We want you to remain the guy who fights for our values, protects our pocketbooks, and explains us to Washington rather than explaining Washington to us." Here we were, only two and a half hours into the majority, and already I was beginning to get a taste of how challenging it might be.

By three in the morning, it was obvious we would be the first Republican majority in forty years. Reporters immediately began asking me what we would do now that we were in charge. "Implement the Contract," I said. The more sophisticated weren't satisfied. "Look, the election is over," they said. "Can you tell us what you are *really* going to do now that you've won your victory?" Each time I would pull out my copy of the Contract. "Read this," I told them.

CHAPTER 10

Implementing the Contract: Part I

After months of planning, we were ready to take over the House on Wednesday morning, November 9. We had already scheduled a senior-staff conference call, a senior-planning-group conference call, and a leadership conference call for the first day after the election. Now we were simply executing the first phase of the plan. Overall it worked remarkably well and was a good omen for the future. We appointed Jim Nussle to head a transition team and gave him a strong group of aggressive younger members to help. Our opening agenda was to audit the House, cut committee staffs, and shrink the general size of the legislative branch.

In retrospect, one key decision was to pick several committee chairmen outside the seniority system. Bob Livingston, Tom Bliley, and Henry Hyde became chairmen of Appropriations, Commerce, and Judiciary even though they did not have seniority. In each case, I thought they would bring a level of aggressiveness and risk taking that we would need in these very important positions. I was frankly surprised at the powerful positive reaction to these choices. For almost a year, we had been talking about reform from the ground up, yet people seemed surprised when we actually started to follow through.

Another major change was to eliminate and alter several committees. David Dreier of California led the task force on this issue. He concluded that several committees were no longer necessary, while others needed to be reorganized or renamed. The Merchant Marine and Fisheries Committee, the District of Columbia Committee, and the Post Office and Civil Service Committee all disappeared. The Energy and Commerce Committee, which John Dingell had turned into an empire, lost railroads and part of its energy jurisdiction. Other committees were renamed and refocused. The Armed Services Committee became the National Security Committee and Government Operations became Government Reform. Our aim was to rethink the entire size and structure of the Congress.

At our organizing conference in December, a number of key positions were hotly contested. DeLay was elected whip by a small margin over Bob Walker, even as both of them were working in the strategic planning group preparing for opening day. We agreed beforehand that whoever lost the whip race would chair the leadership meetings. John Boehner became conference chairman and Chris Cox, a brilliant Californian who had been deputy counsel to the President in the Reagan White House, became the policy chairman.

Susan Molinari won conference vice chair and Barbara Vucanovich was elected secretary of the conference—the first two women to serve in the elected leadership of either party. Jan Meyers of Kansas and Nancy Johnson of Connecticut also chaired House committees (Small Business and Ethics). This was the first time there were two chairwomen at the same time. Robyn Carl was chosen clerk of the House and Cheryl Lau (an Asian American) became House counsel—the first two women to serve as officers of the House.

We also established a bipartisan Committee on the Family

chaired by Congressman Frank Wolf. We found both members and their spouses eager to participate, and a number of Democratic members were also enthusiastic about trying to make Congress a more humane environment. It may seem like a small thing, but having a chaotic schedule can make congressional life very difficult. Failing to plan recesses so they coincided with children's school vacations had made family life hard to preserve. My wife, Marianne, participated enthusiastically in the sessions of Frank Wolf's committee. With the intense time pressures we had set for ourselves, it was clear we were going to have a lot of tired members and staff at the end of three months.

Three practical steps made Congress a little more family friendly. First, we guaranteed that we would always end our sessions by three o'clock on Fridays so members could catch planes home for the weekend. Coincidentally, this allowed members to purchase airline tickets in advance, saving Congress $5 million in the process.

Second, we cut the one hundred days to ninety-three when someone realized that most children had their school vacation the week of April 10. Technically, the one hundred days didn't end until April 13. This earlier recess made our job harder, but it meant that families would have some time together around Easter and Passover.

Third, we announced that floor votes would end after seventeen minutes. Under House rules, the votes must last at least fifteen minutes but can actually stay open as long as the chair desires. In the last several Congresses, the Democratic leadership became more and more indulgent and votes grew longer and longer. One vote actually lasted forty-nine minutes while the chair waited for several members to show up. Wolf's Committee on the Family calculated that nearly a week could be saved simply by insisting on a seventeen-minute limit. Since Congress votes eight hundred or more times per session, the savings would be fifty-three hours. Members quickly adjusted to the new rules and everyone has been happy with the result.

We developed other ways to make Congress more friendly to family life. We turned the Tip O'Neill Room just off the House chamber into a family room, which is now widely used by spouses and family friends. We invited the Power Rangers to the opening day. I am not a big Power Ranger fan, but for the very young it was the equivalent of inviting the four presidents on Mount Rushmore. One freshman, J. D. Hayworth of Arizona, said his four-year-old daughter didn't want to fly to Washington to see her dad sworn in until she heard that the Power Rangers would be on hand. Then flying in an airplane seemed okay. Of such little building blocks is a more family-friendly Congress made.

Opening day was obviously about much more than the Power Rangers. We had pledged ourselves to nine reforms in the first session—a huge workload under any circumstances. Our side had not had anyone sitting in the Speaker's chair for forty years. None of the current Republican members had ever attempted to move legislation through the House. It was certainly going to be a challenge.

We were nervous because no one had any real idea how the Democrats would react. We knew they had promised to oppose many of our reforms. What we didn't know was whether they would simply debate them or use every parliamentary trick in the book to slow business to a crawl. An all-out effort could have tied up ten hours in procedural motions.

Bob Walker, our best floor tactician; Jerry Solomon, our Rules Committee chairman; and Tom DeLay, our elected whip, held training sessions that rehearsed every motion of the first day, step by step. Our freshmen members went through scripting and practice before they were even sworn in. There were practice sessions on the floor of the House during December (the Democrats still technically controlled the House until January 4 but were more than considerate and gave us every opportunity to prepare). Republicans played the roles of Barney Frank, David Bonior, and other Democratic opponents. We needed the experience. Only one member of the House, Sid Yates of Illinois, was in office in 1954, the last time the Republicans had a majority—and he is a Democrat.

All this practice paid off on an opening day that was the longest in history and virtually flawless. Congressman Bill Emerson of Missouri organized an ecumenical prayer service at a nearby Catholic church for members and their families. Both Democratic and Republican members participated. Frank Wolf gave a particularly powerful sermonette on the spirit of reconciliation. I was so moved that I resolved to rethink my speech for the swearing-in ceremony.

After the service, we went to the Capitol, where the roll was called and a quorum reported. This is always time-consuming, so I spent time in the Speaker's office getting my picture taken with Georgians who had come in for the big day. When the quorum is established, the two party leaders' names are put into nomination for Speaker. This is a formality, since everyone knows who has the votes, but there is a drama in going down the list of names. Each member shouts out "Gephardt" or "Gingrich." The first three members were Democrats and when they had voted another Democrat called out, "I move the vote be closed." The House broke up in laughter. My five- to nine-year-old nieces and nephew were sitting on the floor at the back of the House and began getting worried when they kept hearing Gephardt votes. Finally, one of our members leaned over and assured them that Uncle Newt would win.

While the vote was proceeding, I went to the Speaker's ceremonial office and outlined a more conciliatory, bipartisan speech. As I finished, Dick Gephardt came by. Marianne and I have become good friends with Dick and Jane, but I knew it was going to be painful for him to escort me to the rostrum, as tradition dictates. It was always painful for us watching Bob Michel turn over the gavel to the Democratic Speaker. After forty years of uninterrupted rule, the process would be even more emotionally difficult for the Democrats. With the enthusiasm and determined cheerfulness that are his trademark, Dick bantered for a minute and then we walked to the door of the House. My name was announced and the members began giving me a standing ovation. As I stepped into the chamber, the first people I encountered were my nieces and nephew. It was an emotional moment. I looked up at the gallery, where I knew Marianne and my entire family were seated. They loved seeing me and the kids together at this historic occasion.

I will never forget mounting the rostrum and looking over the House for the first time. It was an amazing experience. Until that moment, I had never actually imagined myself standing there as Speaker. I had seen myself as a leader, but this was a moment for which I was not prepared. The House is a large room and on this day it was filled with over five hundred people on the floor. To my left stood former Congressman John Rhodes, the minority leader when I arrived in Congress. Next to him was Bob Michel, who had served valiantly for so many years as minority leader. Bob Walker and Congressman David Dreier were standing at the front and both had tears running down their faces. Bob Dole had recessed the Senate and he and his Republican colleagues joined us for a moment not seen for forty years. The Democrats were more than polite in their applause. Most of them were gracious and have remained pleasant and conciliatory to this day. The whole scene gave me a wonderful sense of the romance of America and the magic by which Americans share power and accept changes in government. I tried to rise to the occasion in my speech, wanting very much to reach out to the whole House and not be just a partisan Republican leader.

From that point, I had to preside over the House during an initial fight over the rules. At about three in the afternoon I stepped down to participate in other activities. The most amazing thing to me was that our planning and training had been so thorough that from then until two the next morning, I never thought about what was happening on the House floor. I knew that Armey, DeLay, and Walker had everything under control. I could focus on my job while they performed theirs.

Because of the historic circumstances, a huge number of House freshmen wanted to bring their families to the ceremonial office for a photograph. That afternoon we took pictures with 108 members, with more than a thousand people participating. It was a happy day and the feeling was reinforced that night as I attended a gala filled with five thousand happy Republicans partying at the new Congress's inception.

On January 5, we began work on the Contract. Dick Armey was chief operating officer while I was chief executive and chairman of the board. This division of labor allowed me to focus on long-range planning while Dick focused on the day-to-day operations. I do not know if anyone ever used this division of responsibilities before in the Congress, but it sure worked for us.

The House has a complicated system for bringing bills to the floor. First a subcommittee has to mark up a bill, then it is reported to the full committee. When the full committee calls a meeting, it has to give notice to the minority members. After the markup, the minority gets three full days to write a report offering dissenting views. A similar procedure then takes place in the Rules Committee. Every bill has to have a rule that sets its procedures before it comes to the House floor. The only two exceptions are when something is brought up under unanimous consent or in a process called a suspension when the House by two-thirds vote decides to suspend the rules and pass something. I outline this to illustrate that passing anything through the House is a complex business and takes time.

Dick Armey's assignment was to outline a path for passing the ten major proposals of the Contract (that eventually became thirty-one bills when written in detail). With only ninety-three days allotted, he did not have much margin for error.

One of the most amazing aspects of the one hundred days was the narrowness of our majority. In recent years, Democrats have had about 240 to 260 votes. That meant they could lose a dozen members and still win without a single Republican vote. The great one hundred days of FDR involved a Democratic majority of over 300.

Our margin was much slimmer. We were trying to push through a major reformation of government with a majority of twelve votes. At any moment, a loss of thirteen Republicans could have ended the effort.

Tom DeLay, the new whip, and Denny Hastert, his chief deputy, were the ones who had to worry most about lining up the votes. While Armey was overseeing the legislative flow, Tom and Denny were working behind the scenes to ensure that we would have a majority every time it counted. On a couple of occasions, it got real close.

Tom believes in what he calls "growing the vote." His idea is to listen to every member and understand what they need so that they can comfortably vote for a bill. He brings together grass-roots activists and informed members to build a team that backs the idea as it comes to the floor. Tom and Denny did it brilliantly for the Contract. The problem was that we were tackling so many ideas so rapidly, we were often too busy with the last vote to have time to grow the next.

As the weeks went by and members became more tired, the stakes grew higher. We had deliberately put the easiest votes early so we could practice with minimum risk. This enabled us to win early victories and build momentum. But it also left the hardest votes for when we would be most exhausted.

At the beginning, Bill Clinger of Pennsylvania, chairman of the Government Reform Committee, got us off to a great start with a long debate and series of contested amendments on the unfunded mandate reform bill. This was a very popular bill deeply desired by state and local governments. It was clearly going to pass, but liberal Democrats kept Clinger on the floor for days as they offered amendment after amendment. Clinger good-naturedly continued to plug away and after a while the Democrats relented. The bill passed by a large margin.

This is important because it is rarely reported by the news media. Again and again the Democrats would try to undermine or delay a bill through procedural moves but then vote for it on final passage. They knew there was too much popular support for them to be on the record in opposition. But they did their best to gut these bills anyway in little-noted proceedings. That's one reason why Democrats have gotten away with so many things for so long—and why open-door technologies such as C-SPAN have done so much to improve Congress.

The committee chairman with the hardest job was Jerry Solomon, the Rules Committee leader. Solomon is a tough ex-marine from upstate New York. Every bill has to go through the Rules Committee and this gives the minority an opportunity to make things as difficult as possible. Since Solomon had done the same thing as the ranking minority member in the old Congress, he knew what was coming. Only once in thirteen weeks did he need my help in getting a bill out of committee—and that was with the difficult welfare reform bill.

The second-hardest committee assignment was the Judiciary Committee, chaired by Henry Hyde of Illinois. In a few short weeks, Henry produced two constitutional amendments (balanced budget and term limits), three litigation reform bills, and five crime bills. It was a herculean challenge, complicated by the aggressive and articulate opposition of Barney Frank, Charles Schumer, and Pat Schroeder. Henry's effort was particularly heroic because he reported out the term limits amendment while being personally opposed to it—as he expressed in a widely quoted speech in the House. It was an extraordinary display of principle and courage to get all those bills out of one committee in such a short time.

The third effort was on the Ways and Means Committee chaired by Bill Archer. Ways and Means has jurisdiction over the tax code and is arguably the most important committee in the House. Certainly Wilbur Mills and Danny Rostenkowski thought so. Archer, quiet and reserved, had been our ranking minority member but—like all of us—had never chaired a committee. Now he blossomed as a leader. Every day Archer seemed to grow as he accepted responsibility and authority. He produced a welfare reform bill that satisfied several key constituencies while still managing to retain its historic proportions. No reform effort of recent years fit the values of the country more than this bill. The bill insists on work requirements, strengthens the family, reestablishes male responsibility for children, and discourages young girls from getting pregnant outside marriage. By the time the bill passed the House, one poll showed 96 percent of the country favored replacing the current welfare system—a unanimity virtually unknown on any other issue.

CHAPTER 11

Implementing the Contract: Part II

For all its popularity, welfare reform nonetheless came the closest of any Contract issue to collapsing (except of course term limits, which failed to get the two-thirds vote needed to pass the House). Our problem was not the other party. There were enough Democrats eager for welfare reform to ensure final passage. Our problem was those Republicans who were reluctant enough about the bill to defeat the rule that would be necessary to bring the bill to the floor. The result was that we split over the rule. We were in danger of not having a majority on our side (we needed 218 and with only 230 members any 13 could defeat us). In addition, even conservative Democrats who backed welfare reform were tired of having Republicans win on every issue and were ready to desert us if they sensed we couldn't round up the votes.

As a result, instead of getting the twenty-odd Democrat votes we would normally expect on the rule, we got only three. That meant we could not afford to lose more than fifteen

Republicans. We had already lost two Cuban-American Republicans who wouldn't support the ban on welfare for legal immigrants. Other Republicans were irritated by the closed rule that had been reported. They wanted an amendment made in order to allow them to take out one of the anti–teen pregnancy provisions.

Then the bombshell exploded. The Catholic Conference of Bishops and the National Right to Life organization both decided they would oppose welfare reform because it might lead to more abortions.

No other right-to-life groups agreed and the majority of conservative analysts disputed the Bishops and National Right to Life on their conclusions. Marvin Olasky pointed out in a thoughtful *Wall Street Journal* article that curbing the epidemic of teenage pregnancies was just as likely to lead to a *reduction* in abortions since without the financial support of the government young people were less likely to engage in casual sex. But that didn't help us now.

Between them, these two organizations could probably carry away thirty or more votes. We had no way to compromise because other profamily and conservative social groups were just as adamantly convinced that the bill would lower the number of abortions. It wasn't a matter of being pro- or antilife, but a question of interpreting the effects that government incentives were having on people's behavior. In a final irony, Harold Volkmer, a right-to-life Democrat, joined with Pete Stark, an extremely liberal Democrat, to write an amendment that won the support of both the National Right to Life *and* the National Abortion Rights League, surely a first. The amendment would have eliminated the anti–teen pregnancy provisions in a way that allowed the Abortion Rights League to argue that it would increase the current number of abortions while the National Right to Life argued that it would reduce abortions. Both groups were for it with diametrically opposed analysis but great enthusiasm. No wonder people were losing their bearings.

In a whip meeting, most of our hard-core right-to-life supporters were furious at what they saw as a deliberately deceptive strategy to sabotage a reform bill they sincerely believed would reduce abortions. They were ready to pass the rule without giving Volkmer and Stark a vote on their amendment. The energy was there. We just didn't have the votes.

The day before the rules vote, Haley Barbour, Bob Dole, and I had lunch with a dozen key Republican governors who had helped write the welfare reform bill. Their participation had been one of the real secrets of our success. I reported honestly but bleakly that we were in danger of losing the rules vote. As practical leaders who had long dealt with their own legislatures, they had a simple solution. They adjourned the meeting and went up to the Capitol as a group. The six strongest prolife governors—led by John Engler of Michigan, Fife Symington of Arizona, Tommy Thompson of Wisconsin, and Mike Leavett of Utah—all went to Henry Hyde's office to plead with him. He said later that he had never had so much attention in his life and was frankly flattered. (Remember, we had been in the minority for a long time.) With the help of the governors and profamily grassroots activists, we began to shrink the number opposed to the rule. Still, we were about a half-dozen votes behind.

Just before the vote, we held a very emotional meeting with the representatives who were most deeply committed to the right to life. A few said they could help, but most felt they could not leave the Bishops and National Right to Life. One member said if there was any doubt, he had to vote no. He had an adopted son and was haunted by the idea that his child would have been aborted.

When the rules vote began I was on the floor and voted early. Normally the Speaker does not vote, but on this occasion I wanted to indicate how serious the stakes were. I moved around the floor working with Tom DeLay and the whip organization, trying to resolve as many concerns as possible. For a brief moment during the seventeen-minute vote, it looked as if we would lose. Then several Republican moderates switched out of Party loyalty when they saw the conservative Democrats uniting against us. I began to breathe a little easier. Three Democrats kept their commitment and voted with us. Twelve right-to-life Republicans joined the three others in voting against the rule.

We won 217 to 211. A few absent members would have voted with us if we had called on them, but the margin was as narrow as it could get. The Contract had survived its worst test. Once the rules hurdle had been cleared, we passed the most comprehensive welfare reform bill in history by a solid margin.

Our next assignment was the large tax cut promised by the Contract. This included a capital gains tax cut and indexing capital gains against inflation. It also included a repeal of the Clinton tax increase on senior citizens' Social Security and a new American Dream Savings Account that would allow people to withdraw money to buy a first house, help put children through college, or pay medical expenses. In every instance, we were trying to encourage people to save and invest.

Ironically, the most controversial part of the tax bill became the $500-per-child tax credit. This had been adopted with the support of profamily groups and the Christian Coalition, who saw it as a clear gesture of support to families with children. For parents with three children and an income of $40,000 a year, it would mean a $1,500 tax break.

I always thought the issue was very simple. We believe that if you have children and earn money, you ought to have first claim on your money to care for your own children. Our liberal friends believe the bureaucrats deserve the money more than the parents. Liberals generally believe that bureaucrats are so much wiser and more efficient that even after the bureaucrats' salaries and expenses are subtracted, that $500 in the bureaucracy will do much more for the child than in the parents' hands. In sum, the argument was between the family budget and the federal budget. We believe the family budget is primary, the liberal Democrats believe the federal budget comes first.

The great surprise was that the income level at which the child tax credit would be cut off became a big issue. Originally, we had no limit. However, a number of members felt uncomfortable about giving the credit to the very wealthy, and we compromised at $200,000 in joint income. Frankly, setting any limit was probably an error. There is a class warfare mentality that infects the Washington press corps and sets the tone of much of the debate in Washington. For the last three weeks of the Contract, the big issue became whether the Republicans would cave in to class-warfare rhetoric and set a lower cap. This was a much bigger issue than it appeared. Many members were almost eager to lower the cap to $95,000. In part they were motivated by a desire to seem more populist. The battle cry of helping the rich has always caused Republicans to flinch. In addition, there was a certain amount of what Congressman Dick Armey called "Contract compliance fatigue." People were just tired of toeing the line and wanted more free expression and less teamwork. For a few members, it was an opportunity to grandstand for the news media. Since the liberals in the Washington press corps will always play up a Republican who fights other Republicans, there is a certain advantage in breaking with the team.

From my point of view, there were several reasons for not giving in. First, once we allowed a $95,000 cap, a bidding war would open up, with the Democrats trying to drive it even lower. Second, the Christian Coalition and other social conservatives had agreed not to include school prayer, abortion, or any other powerfully divisive issues in the Contract in exchange for the tax break for families. If we lost the tax credit in a bidding war, we would break faith with allies who had patiently waited on one side while we worked on other issues. Third, the Washington press corps was desperate to write a headline proclaiming "Republicans fail." For weeks the "analysis" stories had been predicting we would "disappoint" the American people, even as the news stories told of our success. No matter that we had passed the $187 billion tax cut, lowering the cap would be hailed as a

Republican defeat. Finally, the leadership was not ready to accept defeat just as we stood on the verge of a huge historic success.

We were right. With a last burst of effort, the whip organization and our many grassroots allies put together the votes to pass the bill.

With the tax cut passed, we had completed the Contract with America. Our work was almost done. In a way, that had been the easy part. Now it was time to start balancing the federal budget.

The first opportunity to show our mettle came with the annual adjustments to last year's budget. As the legislative year passes, it usually becomes obvious that some budget projections are wrong. Too much or not enough has been appropriated—although with the Democrats in charge it has usually been not enough. Then there are also emergencies that arise—the Gulf War, the savings-and-loan bailout, a flood in the Mississippi Valley—that demand further appropriations. Recisions (cuts in already appropriated money) are harder to make, on the other hand, since departments and bureaus usually hide any surpluses. This is where end-of-the-year spending sprees come from—the effort of bureaucracies to hide their surpluses and make sure they will be able to ask for more money the next year.

Shortly after taking over in January, we realized we would have to make two emergency appropriations, one for defense and one for the flooding in California. Traditionally, Congress has just waived budget limits and spent the extra money. We, however, saw it as a test of whether we were truly different. Bob Livingston, our newly installed chairman of the Appropriations Committee, decided that he would come up with spending cuts to offset these appropriations. It would be an enormous first step toward fiscal discipline.

When Bob first mentioned the cuts, I thought he was talking in the neighborhood of $6 billion or $7 billion. Then he dropped by the office one night with a huge grin on his face. He announced that he could cut current-year appropriations by *$17* billion. This would pay for all the emergency requests and still save $11 billion for the taxpayer. It would be an enormous achievement.

When Bob first proposed his recision bill, Washington just laughed at us. The Washington media knew that such a bill could not be passed. But the momentum of Livingston's courage caught on and suddenly the mood in the Senate changed. Just before we left for spring recess, the Senate passed a parallel recision bill of almost the same size ($16 billion) by a unanimous 99 to 0 vote. Even President Clinton supported it. Washington's expectations were beginning to change. With Livingston and his appropriators leading the way, we were moving into a new world.

As we enter the long fight to balance the budget by 2002, however, the real workhorse will be John Kasich, the Budget Committee chairman. John is the son of a postman from western Pennsylvania steel country. He is passionately in love with America and deeply determined to live a life that would make his parents proud. They both died in a car crash about ten years ago. His characteristic passion comes in part from grieving and the deep love they showered on him. John may be the most inspirational and creative Republican in Congress. He is a Jack Kemp–type romantic reformer who wants to bring everybody together to do good for the country. John gets along with everybody and has made many friends on the Democratic side.

Kasich's Budget Committee will face the enormous challenge of writing and passing a balanced budget by 2002. During the one hundred days, he warmed up by producing a series of budget changes that proved we could pay for the tax cuts. John came through with flying colors. There were no serious challenges by either the Democrats or the news media as to whether we could pay for the tax cuts. Over the next few years, Kasich will bear the primary responsibility as the House tries to transform the federal government and achieve a balanced budget by 2002. I have no doubt he can do it.

Finally, it was Wednesday night, April 5. Dick Armey asked

me to give the closing speech. As I stood on the floor looking at our members, tears came to my eyes. We had actually done it! With a tremendous team effort, we had kept the Contract in only ninety-one days.

The members also had a kind of solemnity that comes on the last day of the school year. People felt that they were part of a team and were now becoming part of history. We had been through a long, hard epic. Now it was time to relax before girding ourselves for the even greater tasks that lay ahead.

On Friday morning, we went back to the Capitol steps for a celebration of our great effort. That night I spoke to the country on prime-time television. No Speaker of the House had ever done this before. I talked about our accomplishments, but I talked more about the challenges that lay ahead—about our next concerns—balancing the budget, saving Medicare, and preserving the baby boomers' Social Security. Then I flew home and worked Saturday morning on my Habitat for Humanity house. On Sunday, I appeared on *Face the Nation*, spoke at a local synagogue, and spent an hour as a guest on Ross Perot's radio talk show.

On Monday morning, I was sleeping late for the first time in weeks when my dreams were interrupted by a phone call. Congressman Nathan Deal, a colleague from Georgia's Ninth District, wanted me to know that at 10:00 A.M. he was announcing his withdrawal from the Democratic Party. He hoped the Republican Conference would welcome him. I said we would be honored to have him. In 1990 I was again the only Republican congressman among Georgia's eleven representatives. Now there are eight Republicans and three Democrats. It is a promising start for the next phase.

With that phone call, my vacation ended quickly. It was time to start working on balancing the budget and renewing America. With Nathan's conversion, we now had a fourteen-vote margin. What more could you want on a spring morning in Georgia?

PART FOUR

The Ongoing
Revolution

CHAPTER 12

Learning Versus Education

We are confronted today by the most abundant information resources and technologies in the history of the world. Yet Americans now face an unprecedented learning crisis. Poor children enter school with inadequate preparation and are behind from day one. Too many children simply will never learn how to read or write. High school students are not learning the math and science they need to be competitive in the world market. Going to college has become an expensive ordeal that can permanently shatter a family's finances. Finally, our adults are simply unprepared for the level of learning required by new jobs and career developments.

We spend much more on an education system that is producing much less. We double and redouble our efforts even as the system grows more out of touch with the society it is trying to educate.

This tragedy reminds me of the old story about a drunk who is trying to find his car keys under a streetlight. "Where did you lose your keys?" asks a sympathetic passerby. "Back in the alley," the drunk replies. "Then why are you looking here under the light?" the stranger asks in some bewilderment. "I can see better out here," the drunk replies.

Let us start with a simple question: Is our real goal to build an educational system or is it to have people actually learn? Many people feel their college years have been wasted. Others have learned an immense amount without much formal education. Among them are Bill Gates, the founder of Microsoft, Steve Jobs, the founder of Apple computers, and Jack Horner, one of the world's leading paleontologists, all of whom never received a college degree.

The problem begins with this distinction. *Education* describes a system of teachers and students that has grown inefficient and expensive. *Learning* describes a dynamic community of people using whatever means they have to improve their performances and better their lives.

Our failing is that we keep seeking *education* rather than *learning*. We invest more time and money in an old industrial-era, Second Wave school system because we believe that that is where the answers are to be found. It is a sad irony that our sincere commitment leads only to a deepening frustration.

Education has now shrunk into a professional, structured system where a great deal of money is spent on smaller and smaller results. The more we rely on credentials, the more paperwork we create to monitor and control teachers, the more we drive out the missionary spirit and excitement that is at the heart of learning.

We need the courage to start anew. We need the determination to abandon the assumptions of the past and begin creating a Third Wave Information Age learning system that is as different from the current bureaucratic model as the space shuttle is from an 1845 stagecoach.

There are five major distinctions between Second and Third Wave education. They are:

1. Lifetime learning versus a segmented system
2. Learner-focused versus teacher-focused education

3. Achievement versus process as a measure of success
4. Society-oriented approach versus isolated systems
5. Technology-embracing versus technology-averse learning

The Learner Versus the Student

In the Industrial Age, the education model has been a passive student dominated by an active teacher. The teacher is supposed to know (1) what is appropriate to teach and (2) when it is appropriate to teach it. Industrial-Age education is segmented into curriculum blocks and most learning takes place inside a public building. The student's interests are subordinated to whatever the state or national system of experts decree. All students are assumed to learn at the same time and pace. Everything is measured by how many days a student attends school (the usual basis for state and federal aid) and how many credit hours are amassed.

The Third Wave model is remarkably different. First, it assumes the learner is a complex human being endowed with energy and intelligence. Responsibility is placed on the learner rather than on the teacher. Learning is seen as a lifetime process. People will need to learn different things at different levels of mastery at different periods of their lives. The entire society is a platform for learning. Educators are coaches and guides who help learners find their way.

Lifetime Learning Versus a Segmented System

Changes in fields like science and medicine will require that people learn throughout their lives. No job is truly permanent anymore. People will have to learn new skills and renew old ones even when their jobs are seemingly safe and stable. Constant changes in tax laws and government regulation, scientific advances, and breakthroughs by global competitors will oblige everyone to keep constant track of new developments.

Clearly, much lifetime learning occurs outside traditional classrooms. Consider the rise of highly paid corporate consultants who hold brief, intense seminars for top managers. Their customers have very specific information needs. In return, consultants are expected to deliver highly refined information in a short period of time. Professional learners will become intense users of audiotapes, computer networks, and CDs. They will be spending hours in cars and airplanes and will learn to use the time accordingly.

Age doesn't matter. Professional learners measure their success by what they achieve rather than by what credentials they have. Can they use the new computer? How much German can they pick up in six months? Do they understand how to keep the books for the new business? That is their approach.

Contrast this with the pace of bureaucratic, credentialed education. Our children are told they are "ahead of the class." They are promised that the curriculum will be more interesting "next year." They get promoted for the good of their self-esteem, even when they have really not mastered the material.

Children are not so easily fooled. Often children enter school with high hopes and excitement. Within a few years they have lost that spunk. Their drive has been reduced to sullen resentment. They drop out psychologically long before they drop out physically. A major reason is the lockstepped pace of education.

Not long ago, the *McGuffey's Reader* was the prime instrument of education in America. The book was extraordinarily hard by modern standards. It presented real morals and real values taught in the context of a compelling story. After two generations of "blanding out and dumbing down," our reading texts offer as much diversion as a skim through the phone book. They aren't hard to read, but who wants to try?

Children should be encouraged to read whatever interests them at the highest level of complexity they can master. Youngsters who read well should be encouraged to help their fellow students. Forget what the "experts" say. Let's allow our students to be challenged.

Learner-Focused Versus Teacher-Focused Education

Imagine that you woke up this morning and decided to learn something entirely new for your job, a hobby, or simply to enhance your personal skills.

Your first step would be to figure out what related information you already possessed. Then you would need to assess the most efficient way to acquire this new material. If you have been doing a lot of learning you could probably make these two assessments in a matter of minutes. You might do this entirely on your own—like thumbing through the Yellow Pages.

But in a learner-focused society you would have other options, such as calling upon the services of a learning counselor. This might be at the public library, a school system, or your corporation. Or your counselor might be a freelancer, much like training instructors and psychological counselors today. With his or her guidance, you could consider a variety of learning tracks and the possibility of blending them together into a personalized learning plan.

In a learning society your choices might range from a class taught in a traditional classroom to a counselor-led interaction to an apprenticeship with a true master. You might consult an expert, either by computer bulletin board or diskette, or audio- or videotape. Virtually all of these approaches would be available at your convenience.

A learner-focused system would be lifelong, twenty-four hours a day, three hundred sixty-five days a year. The emphasis would be on the responsibility of the learner. It would resemble a library more than a traditional school. The amount of learning going on would increase while costs would be cut dramatically.

Achievement Versus Process as a Measure of Success

I recently asked a group of college students how many of them could have graduated from high school in three years if there had been an incentive to do so. All of them raised their hands. How many could have gotten out in two years? One-third raised their hands.

Imagine a system so inefficient that one-third of its participants believe they are wasting half their time, and virtually all students believe they are wasting at least 25 percent of their time. That is the inevitable result of counting classroom hours instead of the knowledge learned.

There are two simple reforms that would shift this focus. First, establish a scholarship program in which for every year you graduate ahead of your class with a B or better average, the school district gives you a college or advanced-training scholarship equivalent to 80 percent of what it would have spent in educating you for one more year of high school. If you graduate in three years, you get a one-year scholarship. If you graduate in two years, you get a two-year.

Taxpayers would save 20 percent on each of these unnecessary years in school, while students and their families would save on tuition. The schools would become more learning-oriented as students focused on advancing their lives and getting ahead. Schoolwork would matter, since grades would now have real consequences.

By the same token we might also turn around and say that school districts would have to pay for any remedial education required when their graduates reached college. Giving students diplomas without teaching them anything is fraudulent. If a school system certifies that a person has learned something, it ought to stand behind it.

The minute high schools are made accountable for their graduates, they will have a whole new incentive to educate. If teachers and principals know their pay can be docked for turning out students who cannot read or do math, they will become much more honest and aggressive in insisting that students learn.

Society-Oriented Approach Versus Isolated Systems

One major drawback of our current educational bureaucracy is that its components are so isolated. In a learner-focused system, technology would be available twenty-four hours a day, seven days a week.

Imagine, for example, a virtual reality game in which you could enter an exciting jungle sequence only after passing an exam that involved schoolwork. Would that give your child an incentive to learn? Bell Atlantic has been wiring a school system in Union City, New Jersey. In this largely Hispanic community, the dropout rate has plummeted as students begin to get excited about the technology being brought into their classrooms.

At Carrollton High School in Georgia, where my two daughters graduated, students watch a segment on CNN about the day's events and then develop class material using databases. If there is an earthquake in Kobe, Japan, for example, they will learn about Kobe, earthquakes, emergency assistance, the history of earthquakes, and so forth. The result is a reality-based experience employing research, reading, and writing skills.

This example is just a small taste of the learning potential available throughout our society. There is no reason, for example, that people interested in dinosaurs couldn't have their learning led by Jack Horner of the Museum of the Rockies or take a specialized course from the Smithsonian Institution or the American Museum of Natural History.

Technology-Embracing Versus Technology-Averse Learning

Imagine a society in which first-graders are able to check out their very own laptop as soon as they achieve a minimum standard of reading and writing. Imagine they are encouraged to use it for schoolwork, homework, playing games, sending e-mail.

Further imagine that these first-graders could dial into the National Digital Library—a five-year project just launched by the Library of Congress—in which five million pieces of Americana will soon be available through on-line databases, bulletin boards, and CDs. Eleven hundred Civil War photographs by Matthew Brady, Lincoln's original handwritten copy of the Gettysburg Address, the manuscripts of Scott Joplin, all would be available at the touch of a finger. Now *that* would be something that would motivate kids.

Moving education outside the classroom becomes even more important when we consider adult education. There are three areas that already cry out for reform—the unemployed, those with disabilities, and workers who have suffered serious on-the-job injuries.

Federal unemployment insurance should be immediately transformed into an adult learning program. Unemployment insurance was created to counter cyclical unemployment, which was once considered unavoidable in heavy industries. When steel companies and auto makers routinely expected to go through a recession every few years, they worked with labor unions to develop a tax-paid benefit for those slack times. The factory would be rehiring in a couple of months. In the meantime, steel or auto workers could use their twenty-six weeks of unemployment to go deer hunting and bass fishing.

That world has disappeared. Today's unemployed are not likely to be rehired by the same firm. We should take the money currently paid in federal unemployment insurance and use it to fund adult learning. Our goal should be to say, "We are prepared to help you, but we expect you to use the time to develop new skills and help yourself."

Likewise, disability programs should be recast as adult learning.

In particular, people recovering from job-related injuries on worker's compensation should use the time to learn new skills. The best of the nation's rehabilitation hospitals (such places as HealthSouth, which did Bo Jackson's surgery) have made enormous strides in this direction. The difference in what can be accomplished in these programs is often astonishing.

None of this is likely to happen unless we change course. The average school system today invests less than 1 percent of its budget in technology. By contrast, many major corporations invest over 20 percent. As with all public bureaucracies, it pays—in political terms—to hire people and pay large salaries rather than to invest in time- and labor-saving technology. Employees can always provide the votes to keep the system going. Computers don't vote; people do.

Earning by Learning

The more I studied bureaucratic education, the more I became convinced that the system was approaching learning backward. It relies on bureaucracy, not incentives. It removes people from the world instead of getting them into it.

Seven years ago I helped create a program called Earning by Learning, designed to help poor children learn how to read. The program works because it uses incentives and minimizes bureaucracy.

Basically, we encourage children to read by paying them. Volunteers visit housing projects once a week and counsel the children in their reading. They then offer the children two dollars for every book they read during the next month. When they have read the book, the children must answer a few questions about it. If they fail, they must go back and read it some more.

Note how the goal is achievement rather than process. Earning by Learning does not pay the students by the hour or by the effort. It pays for results.

The program is now operating in seventeen states. The results have been extremely gratifying. Our very first summer in

Villa Rica, Georgia, one eight-year-old girl read eighty-three books in ten weeks. She read to her mother, her grandmother, anyone who would listen. Her dad took a day off from work for her graduation because $166 was too much money for an eight-year-old girl to carry home by herself.

While Earning by Learning normally focuses on second- and third-graders, a few years ago in Jonesboro, Georgia, the local volunteers recruited a fifth-grader whose teeth protruded so badly that he was ridiculed by other children and made to feel isolated. He read fifty-five books that summer. When I visited, I handed him Allen Drury's *Advise and Consent*—hardly a children's book. He read a page out loud with only one word mispronounced. At summer's end, two orthodontists agreed to adjust his teeth for free. They spent two years changing his appearance. With the help of caring volunteers and with his own efforts, he changed his life.

A principal at an elementary school in Nashville, Tennessee, told me that Earning by Learning has had a profound effect on her community: The children were starting to get their illiterate parents interested in reading. Parents were coming in and checking out books so that they could keep up with their children. At another project in Georgia, the volunteers were surprised when attendance kept doubling every week. They finally asked the children how they had heard about the program. "Every day when the ice cream truck comes by, the kids who are reading always had money to buy Popsicles," they said. "We wanted some, too."

As children in other housing projects begin carrying books and reading, the whole psychology of the community begins to change. Suddenly, it is the young readers who are the smart ones. They are making money. The kids who aren't reading feel left out.

I am convinced that for 10 percent of the $7 billion now spent on the Federal Title One Reading Program, we could have a revolution in literacy rates among the poor and change standards of acceptable behavior as well. All we have to do is bypass the bureaucracy and create the right incentives.

A number of people argue that paying children to read is objectionable. They say the benefits of reading should be inherent. The children are doing it for the wrong motives. I have three answers for these critics.

First, many of these poor children grow up in neighborhoods in which all the subliminal psychological and cultural pressures are against reading. We are trying to woo people away from one set of cultural values (physical force, dependency, irresponsible childbearing) and into the more powerful and prosperous values of hard work and education. Incentives give us tremendous leverage with these young people.

Second, these children hear incentives to other behaviors on television and radio every day. Baseball players go on strike even when they are making millions. Basketball and football players and rock stars make big bucks. Lottery winners celebrate their jackpots. Ours is an incentive-driven society. Learning is more important than sports or entertainment, yet there are no incentives attached to it.

Third, virtually every middle-class family I know uses at one time or another incentives to motivate their children to learn more. A new baseball glove, a bicycle, a trip to Disney World— you've probably heard them all. Earning by Learning is trying to help children whose parents and neighbors may not have enough money to offer the same kinds of incentives. The results prove it is worth the effort.

One incident in Douglasville, Georgia, turned me into a revolutionary. At our initial briefing, one child at a housing project said, "You are going to cheat us." Amazed, the volunteers asked him what he meant. "You'll get us to read all summer and then you won't pay us," he said.

That remark convinced me that the welfare state has to be replaced. If an eight-year-old is already so cynical that he expects to be cheated by volunteers trying to help him, then we are in danger of losing another entire generation. My sense of urgency was increased dramatically by that incident.

At other times in history, the family, the workplace, neighbors, friends, and volunteers have played an essential part in education. There is no reason why learning and education should be restricted to the classroom. The unusually high SAT scores of many home-schooled children suggest that learning can take place just as well under these circumstances. Technologies such as computers, CDs, and videotapes that are available to children in school for one hour a week could be available in their homes seven days a week, twenty-four hours a day.

The problem is that most children are trapped in a nineteenth-century model of a factory, where the emphasis is on high human-labor costs and low technological investment. We don't just want to put computers in the schools. We want to redesign the entire learning process to fit the Information Age.

Earning by Learning is a volunteer effort that seeks to remain nonbureaucratic. Don Jones, an entrepreneur from Wisconsin, and Dr. Mel Steely of West Georgia College, are building a nationwide program. If you would like to participate, call Earning by Learning at 800-214-3276.

CHAPTER 13

Individual Versus Group Rights

One of the great debates of the near future will be individual versus group rights. It is a debate that must end decisively in favor of the individual. Our Declaration of Independence tells us we are "endowed by our Creator with certain inalienable rights." If our rights are inalienable, they clearly belong to us as individuals. They cannot be taken away by the government because our Creator outranks the government. Similarly, neither can they be taken away by a group.

The very concept of group rights contradicts the nature of America. America is about the future, about "the pursuit of happiness," while group rights are about the past. America asks who you want to be. Group rights ask who your grandparents were.

America is about a dynamic, shifting, mobile world of opportunity where everyone has a chance to build a better mousetrap or bake a bigger pie. Group rights is a concept that fits a static world in which limited resources have to be carefully allocated by the government.

America is about pulling together, about a constructive, pragmatic vision of creating a better future by immersing our individual energies into a bigger and better team. This is the America of the wagon train, the barn raising, the flag raising on Mount Suribachi, the *Apollo* trip to the moon, the can-do spirit that is at the heart of American history. In America people learn to be open, creative, conciliatory, and positive in their attitudes.

Group rights are about grievances, lawsuits, conflict, and the use of government coercion to impose a solution on an adversarial relationship. Group rights trap us into lawyers, trials, courts, and a suspicious view of one another. Every inconsequential action carries the threat of a complaint, a grievance, an administrative action. People learn to be defensive, cautious, and protective.

America is about each individual seeking happiness and marrying someone he or she falls in love with, then having American children who seek a better future for themselves and their families. In America individuals from an extraordinary range of nationalities can fall in love and marry without stigma and without worrying about the genetic pattern they are creating. In America the goal is for each individual to find the right friends, neighbors, and life partner and together create a more perfect union. The pursuit of happiness is not defined by the group you came from but by the dream you seek and the dreamer you seek it with.

Group rights trap us within our own group. Each association is measured by genes rather than by compatibility. Group rights would reconstitute America into a seething band of competing, legally defined groups maneuvering against one another for governmentally imposed special privileges.

Martin Luther King, Jr.'s greatest speech asserted that there could be a world where his children would be measured by the content of their character rather than by the color of their skin. There has never been a simpler or more eloquent statement of the difference between the American dream and the horrors of caging people into groups for judgmental purposes.

Dr. King was right. America begins with individuals and the endowments of their Creator. Let's keep pursuing that dream.

CHAPTER 14

Illegal Immigration in a Nation of Legal Immigrants

Illegal immigration should be a simple slam-dunk for any serious citizen. The principles that leap out are obvious and historically irrefutable:

First, anything illegal is by definition wrong. We are opposed to illegal drugs, to illegal violence, to illegal immigration. It is against the law, and it should be stopped.

Second, any nation has an absolute obligation to protect its sovereign border. If you can't block people from coming across your border, you really can't protect your citizens.

Third, everyone knows where our border is. As dozens of nations have done before us, we must learn to guard it effectively. The sad reality is that an open border separating a wealthy welfare state from a poor developing country will attract millions of illegal immigrants. It is our duty to have an effectively protected national boundary. It is the federal government's job to see that we do.

Fourth, when people have succeeded in illegally entering the United States there should be a quick and efficient method of deporting them. Hours or days—not months or years—is the correct length of time. Whatever laws need to be changed to make speed and efficiency possible must be changed. The current legal circus encourages illegal immigrants and makes it surprisingly easy for them to stay in the United States for a lengthy period of time.

Fifth, any costs incurred by state and local governments in taking care of illegal immigrants should be reimbursed by the federal government. This is a federal problem. If it costs the federal government money, that will simply provide an incentive for Washington to get its act together and solve the problem.

Sixth, stopping illegal immigration may ultimately require everyone to carry employee identification cards that have holograms or other hard-to-counterfeit devices. The current black market in identity cards makes a mockery of our laws. When the deliberately crooked illegal immigrant can get a green card faster than the deliberately law-abiding legal resident, there is something wrong.

Seventh, we should develop a guest-worker program to allow foreigners to work temporarily in the United States. This may be the safety valve that allows Mexico and its neighbors to accept a tough, decisive United States policy against illegal aliens. The right kind of guest-worker program, modeled on those in effect in Europe, will allow economically aggressive immigrants to come to the United States on a temporary basis, creating a win-win relationship: They contribute to the American economy while taking earnings back to their native country.

Eighth, this much clearer and more aggressively enforced system will also allow us to be more practical and helpful in issuing visitors' visas for people to come to the United States. The long lines at our consulates—the result of our suspicious attitudes—are hurting American tourism. Ironically, we are stopping people who would like to spend their money but not stopping their cousins who want to sneak in and work illegally. We have the worst of both worlds.

Ninth, within this framework we should be as open and enthusiastic as ever about people who want to come to enter America as legal immigrants. Preference should go to immigrants who possess knowledge, skills, and investment capital. We should also favor those who are reuniting immediate (but not extended) families. The open door should remain open.

Finally, we should not knowingly give welfare or government aid to illegal immigrants except for emergency health care. The whole notion of knowingly allowing illegal residents to collect welfare is a sign of just how out of touch the welfare bureaucracy has become.

There is no magic to solving the problem of illegal immigrants. It is not intellectually challenging. Throughout history, countries that have survived have learned to maintain their borders. There are plenty of practical examples of how to get the job done. If we work at it we can dry up 95 percent of illegal immigration within two or three years. Our challenge is getting to a clear decision, developing a workable plan, and implementing it relentlessly.

CHAPTER 15

English as the American Language

Sometime in the 1960s, we were told that since all people and cultures were equal, it was inappropriate for middle-class America to impose the English language on poor people and people from other cultures. The imposition of this racist, colonial way of speaking on young people of other ethnic groups would deprive them of their cultural roots.

There are two problems with this argument. First, at a personal level, it is difficult for a poor person or an immigrant to get anywhere in this country without learning English. There are nearly two hundred different languages spoken in America (sixty alone in one school in my congressional district). Yet nearly all our business, politics, education, and commerce is conducted in English. It's just plain easier to have one standard language than a dozen. Even a country like India, which has hundreds of languages and local dialects, has adopted English as the language of commerce and education. It is liberating when people can understand one another.

A generation ago, African Americans were being held back by racial segregation, much of it officially sanctioned by the government. Then the moment of liberation came. Tragically, it was at that very moment that the educational establishment decided that standard English was no longer necessary and that grammar and spelling skills could be ignored. While this has had a gradual corrosive effect on middle-class students (virtually every employer, including Congress, can tell horror stories about trying to find college graduates who can write effectively), it has been devastating to poor African Americans and their ability to get good jobs.

Learning a language is hard work. Being able to write clearly, converse fluently, and read with comprehension—these are difficult skills that virtually every student (including me) would have liked to avoid. But if they are not learned in childhood, it becomes much more difficult to do so when you are an adult.

When poor children are told that practicing basketball is better than practicing English, they are more than willing to take this advice. Only in later years will they discover that they have literally dribbled away their opportunities for happiness and a good job. If they belong to a gang that ridicules standard English, they may be marked as strange or uppity for speaking well. If no one at home can spell or use grammar correctly, the difficulties are much worse.

The final result is an angry young man who feels that violence is the only way he can express himself, or a young girl who thinks that the only great accomplishment she can achieve in life is to have a baby. Many of the twelve- and thirteen-year-olds now filling our maternity wards cannot read their own children's birth certificates.

The problem is even more acute among first-generation immigrants and their children. Historically, emigrating to America was an exhausting but exhilarating experience. The millions of immigrants who came through Ellis Island hoped to find happiness and give their children a better life, but it was hard work. The new land was a school of hard knocks that compelled every immigrant family to immerse itself in the process of becoming American.

According to the theory of the melting pot, if people had wanted to remain immersed in their old culture, they could have done so without coming to America. Immigrating itself was a reaching out for a new and better future. It expressed a willingness to learn, grow, and change in the pursuit of a better life. It was not uncommon for people to take two or three jobs to make ends meet. People often lived in crowded and unhealthy circumstances. Yet people kept coming to America because the sense of opportunity outweighed the hardship.

Today the counterculture left and its allies profess to smooth the path for immigrants by setting up bilingual education programs, making it possible for children to continue in their own language. In fact, they have actually made it more difficult. Bilingual education slows down and confuses people in their pursuit of new ways of thinking. It fosters the expectation of a duality that is simply not an accurate portrayal of America.

Immigrants need to make a sharp psychological break with the past, immersing themselves in the culture and economic system that is going to be their home. Every time students are told they can avoid learning their new native language (which will be the language of their children and grandchildren), they are risking their future by clinging to the past.

There are also practical problems. With over two hundred languages spoken in the United States, it is physically impossible to set up bilingual education for each one. No school system could possibly afford it. In addition, educators and professionals who make their living running these programs often become the biggest opponents for letting these people move into the mainstream. Sadly, there are some ethnic leaders who prefer bilingualism because it keeps their voters and supporters isolated from the rest of America, ghettoized into groups more easily manipulated for political purposes often by self-appointed leaders.

By time-honored tradition, new American immigrants have joined various friendship societies and fraternal organizations that help maintain the holidays, customs, and cuisines of their ancestral homes. The more immigrants assimilate to America, the more they often want to renew social and fraternal ties with "the old country." We all remember and celebrate our past—but we remain aware that it is the past. We can all honor our racial or cultural identities without assuming this fact alone will inevitably determine all our ideas and our politics. Maintaining one's special identity is perfectly compatible with assimilation into American civilization—indeed is a characteristic of it.

The new multiculturalism takes a much more radical approach. Bilingualism keeps people actively tied to their old language and habits and maximizes the cost of the transition to becoming American. As a result, poor Americans and first-generation immigrant children have suffered pain and confusion.

Yet the personal problems caused by bilingualism are over-shadowed by the ultimate challenge they pose to American society. America can absorb an amazing number of people from an astonishing range of backgrounds if our goal is assimilation. If people are being encouraged to resist assimilation, the very fabric of American society will eventually break down.

Every generation has two waves of immigrants. One is geographic—we call them "immigrants." The other is temporal—we call them "children." A civilization is only one generation deep and can be lost in a very short time. Insisting that each new generation be assimilated is the sine qua non of our survival.

The only viable alternative for the American underclass is American civilization.

Without English as a common language, there is no such civilization.

CHAPTER 16

Health Care as an Opportunity in the World Market

When the Clinton administration tackled health care, it argued that bringing down medical costs was the way to balance the federal budget. It soon ended up arguing that we have too many specialists, too many MRI machines, and too much high technology. Limiting the number of doctors in specialties, cutting down on investment, and persuading doctors and hospitals to practice a more old-fashioned type of medicine became the goals of the Clinton health plan.

This is a remarkably backward approach. For the last two decades we have been moving through a series of medical breakthroughs that are making America the center of worldwide medicine. The complaint has been that these breakthroughs are too expensive and are giving us medicine we can't afford. But that is the fault of our bureaucracy and our confused insurance system. No one considers the foreign-exchange value of these developments and their ability to help us compete in a worldwide market.

There are five forces moving us toward becoming the great, prosperous center of worldwide medicine.

First, we are entering the age of molecular medicine. Breakthroughs in our understanding of DNA are having an astonishing effect on our ability to treat the human body. From the mechanical focus of nineteenth-century anatomy to the chemical focus and microbiological approach of the twentieth century, we are now entering an era when doctors may be able to work directly on the human gene. This means that previously incurable diseases such as cystic fibrosis, diabetes, and certain inherited cancers may now be treatable. There are a variety of "orphan diseases"—obscure genetic conditions that force people to lead very restricted lives—that may soon be curable through genetic surgery. These techniques will make us a world magnet for medical treatment in the twenty-first century.

Second, computers are allowing us to sort and store more data and to build more sophisticated systems. Soon we will be able to network knowledge from all over the world. Medical analysts in almost any country will be able to interface with the state of the art in hundreds of fields. Today, we are close to 5 percent of the way into this system, but it could become fairly common within two decades. With work, we could make it in five years.

Eventually, your local doctor will be able to diagnose your case by consulting a world database. The doctor would find who is doing the most work in that field and where the most advanced research is being pursued. Patients with rare diseases and parents of children with orphan conditions will rapidly become experts in the field. We will have a better informed public, lower costs, and a system that will be very attractive to foreigners. Actually, a large number of Canadians are already coming to American doctors and hospitals because they cannot get advanced treatment in Canada's socialized medical system.

Third, the explosive growth in our ability to communicate by satellite and fiber optics is creating an entirely new realm of telemedicine. The army is a pioneer in this area. It wants the wounded soldier on the battlefield to have access to the best brain surgeon in the world if that will save his or her life. The most isolated rural hospital will soon have access to the best medicine in the world. Computer networks will bring together the best international experts, who will consult from their home offices. Experiments are under way in which surgeons practice their craft in virtual reality. They will have been through an entire procedure many times over before they finally step into the operating room.

The next wave of investment will be in satellite uplinks that allow the transmission of so much data that it is almost the same thing as being there. Surgeons may one day be able to operate by remote control. American doctors and hospitals will be called upon to operate on people in India. We will be able to sell our expertise in every corner of the world.

Fourth, the cost of transmitting information is dropping rapidly as more and more people are being wired into a world-wide market. In just a few years you may be able to consult global databases with the same ease that you now flip through *TV Guide*. The child of a friend of mine was recently afflicted with a rare orphan disease. My friend is a computer buff, and he was soon in conversation with doctors and libraries in Boston, London, Rome, and Zurich. The Internet is the forerunner of a worldwide system that will allow people to track down the best research, the best therapy, the best doctor, and the best hospital. All of this means a growing consumer market for our medical expertise.

Finally, the cost of transportation is dropping almost as rapidly as the cost of information. Northwest Airlines flies a Boeing 747 every weekend from Tokyo to Minneapolis so that Japanese consumers can shop at the Mall of the Americas. If people like our clothing stores and boutiques, what will they think of our heart, liver, lung, and kidney treatments?

This was driven home to me recently when King Hussein of Jordan visited Washington. After appearing at the Capitol, he mentioned that he was headed the next day to the Mayo Clinic to receive his annual checkup. Already our world-class facilities attract an amazing number of people from other countries. Our unmatched facilities and cutting-edge research are a natural attraction to foreign dignitaries and wealthy people overseas. Yet to my knowledge there has never been an intensive effort to market American health care around the world.

By offering the best products, the best therapies, the best experts, and the best clinics and hospitals in the world, we have a dramatic opportunity to increase our foreign-exchange earnings. Much of this will be sold entirely via worldwide satellite and computer communications. Other people will come to the United States for care. We may have a sales force traveling the planet selling American medicine.

Health products and services could be our largest single source of foreign exchange in the twenty-first century. What we regarded only recently as a huge liability may turn out to be our biggest asset. That is what comes from taking problems and turning them into entrepreneurial opportunities.

CHAPTER 17

Health Care as an Opportunity Rather Than a Problem

We stand on the edge of three revolutions in health care. Their combined effect will lower costs, increase quality, and extend opportunities to virtually all Americans.

These three revolutions are:

1. A restructuring of the insurance system to increase flexibility and create new incentives for lower cost care
2. A shift in responsibility and information away from professional guilds and public bureaucracies and toward the individual consumer-citizen
3. An entrepreneurial and scientific revolution that will lower health costs for more and more patients

The computer industry is a good parallel for health care. Forty years ago, the computer industry was dominated by a few large companies producing a small number of expensive machines for a limited number of consumers. The average person could only access a computer by working with a highly skilled professional in a central location.

Then a group of unknown entrepreneurs in small factories and garages developed a series of innovations that transformed the industry. Today millions of people routinely pull out laptops and interact with computers without professional help. They can access a freestanding, worldwide information system that has no central point of command.

No government could have planned this system. In fact, an active government, in collaboration with the few older companies, probably would have done everything it could to put roadblocks in the way. If there had been a Federal Computing Administration, as there are today a Health Care Financing Administration and a Food and Drug Agency, we would probably still be reading about laptops but we surely would not be using them.

Today's insurance industry and health care delivery system are in the same position as the computer industry was forty years ago. They are large centers of power that charge high costs to individuals without leaving them much alternative. Our job should be to allow innovation and the free market to bring costs down while increasing choice and quality. Just as we tell Yeltsin and the Russians to dismantle their centralized command bureaucracies, so we should tell ourselves the same thing.

One lesson we have learned is that we cannot change health care through one big legislative "fix"—as the Clinton administration so disastrously attempted. Such a one-shot cataclysmic effort is bound to fail. Instead, by sensibly building one block at a time, we stand the chance of making dramatic improvements in health care.

There are several specific steps we can take immediately. Each will improve the situation. Together, they can bring us closer to the kind of health care that will benefit every American.

One. We should pass a bill eliminating all preconditions for people who already have insurance.

This happens most often when people change jobs and find themselves unable to take their health insurance with them. Portability is people's biggest insurance concern. All the major companies say it would be very easy to guarantee portability. Such a law would ensure coverage for 85 percent of all Americans.

New York State is an example of how *not* to pass such a law. In an effort to guarantee universal coverage, New York recently passed legislation saying that people could not be denied coverage for preexisting medical conditions *even if they didn't already have insurance.* What they discovered is that everybody started waiting until they got sick before buying insurance. No insurance system can survive under this condition.

Two. Antitrust laws should be changed so that local hospitals can develop specialties and purchase expensive new equipment in concert.

Currently, all hospitals—public, private, and nonprofit—are subject to antitrust laws. They are also supervised by complex state licensing boards, which attempt to "manage competition" among them.

The system is a perfect example of bureaucratic planning that becomes wasteful and guarantees misallocation of resources. Communities have to convince these boards that they need new hospitals. Hospitals have to prove that they need new equipment. Since these boards are inherently political, some groups and communities always win out while others are likely to lose. The result is that medical experts spend thousands of hours in committee meetings trying to protect their interests.

There are two hospitals directly across the street from each other that serve many of my constituents (Northside and Scottish Rite Children's Hospital). In a rational world, they would be able to sit down and plan together in making multimillion-dollar investments. Their doctors and their patients could share resources and technology. But antitrust laws and licensing board supervision does not allow such rational behavior.

In the age of automobile and aircraft travel, it is silly to assume that a local group of hospitals could combine to produce a monopoly. If one community's hospitals tried to gouge its citizens, people would go to neighboring communities. As we develop a national information system for health, the marketplace will offer even more opportunities for comparison shopping.

Eliminating antitrust restrictions on local hospitals and freeing them up to do what works is a first step toward a more rational, innovative system.

Three. Medical savings (Medisave) accounts should be encouraged to make intelligent health care consumers.

Today more than 75 percent of all medical costs are paid by third parties, either insurance companies or the government. This encourages both patients and doctors to squander money. Patients want the most extensive health care possible no matter what the costs. If this means going to the doctor every time a child has the sniffles, who cares? The insurance company is paying. Doctors and hospitals are happy to oblige. The more health care people consume, the more income doctors and hospitals make. Only the third parties—the insurers and the government—try to control costs.

As a result, these third parties end up micromanaging the system. Medicare and Medicaid rules end up dictating what treatment people will get. Doctors complain that they can't make the simplest decisions—deciding on a course of treatment or prescribing medicine—without getting on the phone and consulting the insurance company.

Medical savings accounts would solve the problem. Instead of open-ended coverage, each member of an employee insurance plan would get a three-thousand-dollar annual account. (Self-employed people could start their own accounts, as with a Keogh account.) If you don't use the entire three thousand dollars, you can roll it over to next year, or transfer it to a retirement account, or take it as a year-end bonus. If your medical expenses exceeded three thousand dollars, you would kick into a special "catastrophic" program that would work just like regular insurance. Since people would be spending their own money, they would shop comparatively and spend more wisely.

At *Forbes* magazine and the Golden Rule Insurance Company, Medisave accounts have recently been established. They have already achieved very large savings in medical expenses. When people spend their own money for health care, they turn out to be very frugal shoppers. This reduces the demand on health services and brings prices down for everyone else as well.

Every American ought to have the opportunity to belong to a Medisave system.

Four. We should maximize people's opportunities to buy health insurance at group rates.

Everyone knows that the more people pool together in a health insurance plan, the lower everyone's average costs will be. One of the problems facing people who become unemployed is that they lose their employer-provided group insurance and have to buy individual or family insurance. Since the risk pool is much smaller, they suddenly have much higher insurance costs exactly when they can least afford it. Solving the problem of portability and preconditions doesn't solve the problem of grouping.

We should establish the easiest possible group system so that your church, synagogue, or mosque, trade group, neighborhood, extended family, hobby group, or any other association can form a health-care-buying coop. People will begin to sort themselves into the kind of group insurance they want.

Cleveland, Ohio, has a group insurance plan for small businesses that has had remarkable success in lowering insurance rates for small businesses. We should foster programs like this everywhere. People will pay less and worry less about their health insurance in a system of universal, easy grouping.

Five. All citizens ought to be allowed to take their insurance coverage as cash and spend it on their own insurance and get the same tax break as if their employer had bought it for them.

By an accident of policy, most Americans now get their health insurance through their employer. During World War II, wartime wage and price controls prevented large companies from giving wage increases. To compensate, companies invented the "fringe benefit"—usually an employer-paid health insurance plan. Nearly two-thirds of Americans now get their health coverage from their employers.

The advantage for employers and employees alike is that benefits are tax free. Instead of giving employees a pay raise—40 percent of which may go to the government—big companies can give their employees generous health benefits that have no tax deductions. The drawback is that these "first-dollar" plans (no deductibles or employee contributions) encourage people to overuse the health system. This drives up medical costs for everyone.

We believe that Americans should have the option of taking their health benefits as a cash payment with no tax consequences. As more and more employers move to managed care—with its limitations on where their employees can go for medical care—an increasing number of people may prefer to buy their own coverage. Combined with the Medisave option, this could prove to be quite popular. It would increase citizens' choices in shopping for their health care and free us from the trap of subsidizing overuse of the health care system.

Six. Entrepreneurs will dramatically lower costs by maximizing innovation.

The current tax, regulatory, and third-party payment systems all combine to minimize entrepreneurship in health care. Like defense and education, health care comes close to being a quasi-monopoly run for the benefit of the producers rather than the consumers.

Doctors themselves form a kind of guild, like those of medieval craftsmen. They have their own licensing boards and are constantly trying to limit the number of practitioners and the number of alternative options.

Doctors also act like a trade guild or union in that they want strict job descriptions and don't want other people performing their tasks. Many people have long argued that nurses could perform many of doctors' routine functions in hospitals. But doctors resist these changes because it cuts into their control. The Information Age is now threatening this monopoly—just as the Industrial Age broke down the powers of the medieval guilds.

Government regulation of medicine has also stymied innovation. The Food and Drug Administration is a perfect example. Many drug companies are now moving their research operations abroad because it is so difficult to get a new drug approved by the FDA. Five years and two hundred million dollars are considered an average investment in regulatory approval. Similarly, many Americans are now going abroad to buy drugs that haven't been approved here at home. Orphan diseases are another problem. If you have a rare genetic disease that affects only a few thousand people, it is impossible that the sales of a drug to cure or control it will ever cover the costs of shepherding the drug through the FDA.

All this comes from failing to weigh costs against benefits. The FDA prides itself on the expenses saved when a drug turns out not to work. But it never counts the people who grow sicker and die while waiting for the FDA to approve a drug that *does* work. We need more market forces in the drug business.

From molecular medicine, to computerized expert systems, to telemedicine, to new therapies and ways of organizing existing resources, there are hundreds of opportunities for breakthroughs that will provide better care and more prevention at lower cost. Getting the government out of the way of these innovations is a major challenge of the next few years.

Regina Herzlinger at the Harvard Business School has accurately reported that entrepreneurs are actually lowering the cost of health care through technological and managerial break-throughs. They are responding to market opportunities and offering better and more convenient health care at lower cost. From specialized hospitals that provide one service organized very efficiently, to neighborhood clinics that provide convenience, to new technologies that prevent diseases or minimize the cost of treatment, Herzlinger records success after success in new services that are more desirable and less expensive.

Seven. Market forces have to be strengthened and the citizen's right to be a full customer has to be reestablished.

I tell people in the medical profession that they have two choices. Either they can go the way of Canada or they can go the way of Wal-Mart: They can't stay where they are. What I mean is that if doctors and hospitals keep insisting on telling patients very little, they are going to end up in a Canadian-style government bureaucracy. If they want to retain their freedom, they are going to have to share information with their patients.

Last year my wife developed a thyroid problem. She called several specialists and asked what tests they would recommend and how much they would cost. None of them would tell her anything except that they would be glad to schedule her for an appointment. Marianne was furious at the lack of information and the unnecessary sense of helplessness. This is clearly going to become unacceptable behavior as we move toward a market-oriented health care system.

A recent study of two Pennsylvania hospitals found that one had a much better success rate in operating for heart disease. Amazingly, the good hospital also cost less. In a market-based system, such a situation would never last long. The hospital with high costs and poor outcomes would either improve its operation or lose its customers. By keeping people in the dark, the medical profession is able to avoid responsibility for such inefficiencies.

With the potential of our current information systems, there is no reason not to have a nationwide "medical yellow pages" in which you could check for the specialty you need, the price you will be charged, and the outcome record of the provider. Such a system would probably also include comments from experts and former patients.

It is vital that we establish the citizen's right to be a customer in the medical system. If you are a customer instead of a patient, that means you can ask about price and quality. You can shop around and check your bill intelligently. Just giving people the right to receive a bill they can understand from their doctor or hospital would be a major improvement.

Because health care is now so regulated, there are no competitive pressures to force hospitals and doctors to take these steps. We have to deregulate. If each citizen becomes the primary checker of his or her medical bills, we will see more competitive practices and a dramatic drop in fraud and waste.

Eight. Citizens will become more and more sophisticated as medical systems become easier to understand.

My eighty-year-old mother-in-law is diabetic and uses a home self-diagnosis system every day. She checks herself and varies her insulin according to what her home laboratory tells her. When she was born, such therapies did not exist. Even forty years ago, she would have gone to the doctor's office every day to have her insulin level tested by a nurse. Today she can perform the task at home.

Two doctors recently told me that we could save several billion dollars a year in the treatment of diabetics by shifting to a more educational, prevention-oriented system. Today Medicare will pay for one educational visit to train the diabetic in self-diagnosis but then requires the patient to wait until he or she needs a leg amputated or confronts some other emergency before there can be more government-paid counseling. By minimizing prevention we maximize illness, cost, and suffering.

With the rapid development of expert systems and telemedicine, people's ability to take care of themselves will increase dramatically. Patients will be able to do a lot of self-diagnosis and perform routine care on themselves or on members of their family. They can stay in constant touch with a health professional by phone or a computer network.

With these innovations, much more will be done to liberate people from nursing homes or long-term care. The result will be better for people and their pocketbooks. A lot of professionals will be frightened by this idea of empowering citizens with medical knowledge, but it is the wave of the future. Health care will be more accessible and will save more lives.

Nine. We should reexamine the question of the working poor who are having trouble getting access to health insurance.

We want to ensure that all of our citizens have access to health care. There are a variety of ways to do that. I firmly believe that once the preceding eight steps are in place, insurance costs will be lower and more people will be covered than are today.

Even in the Canadian "universal system," about 3 percent of the population falls through the cracks. These are mostly working people who cannot get coverage at their job but make too much money to qualify for outright government subsidies.

We have an obligation to reassess this part of our society, but we should not do it until all the other building blocks are in place. Once we have a more competitive, consumer-oriented health system, most of these people will be able to get coverage at no extra cost to taxpayers.

Health care offers the American people a tremendous opportunity. We have the best health care in the world—despite all the alarm that has been raised about it in the past few years. Health care should be one of our biggest exports. But it won't happen unless we deregulate the industry and until "patients" are allowed to become "consumers." The technology is already developing. Making health care more advanced and accessible is one of our greatest challenges for the twenty-first century.

CHAPTER 18

Ending the Drug
Trade and
Saving the Children

Future historians who look back on our generation will have a difficult time explaining how we tolerated the invasion of drug dealers and their assault on our children's lives. These historians will have to go back to the counterculture of the late 1960s and its contemptuous dismissal of middle-class values to understand why we have been so ineffective in saving our children from criminals and foreign threats.

The drug epidemic has been the single most destructive development of the last thirty years. It was entirely man-made. There is no magic to understanding drug infestation. Some human beings make a lot of money by helping destroy other human beings. The profits from destroying our children outweigh the potential penalties. Some people are immoral and greedy enough to take the risks. If the cost of their wealth is the destruction of other human beings, so be it.

There are only two questions we have to ask about drugs. First: Do we believe it is undermining our country? Second: Are we prepared to stop it? Surprisingly, the answer among our elites is more ambivalent than you might think.

A considerable number of sophisticated people argue for the legalization of drugs. They are exhausted by the seemingly futile struggle to deal with drug dealers and their violence. They have given up on the underclass and believe that low-cost drugs will eliminate most of the robberies and burglaries that seem to be tied into paying for drugs. They do not think that our society has the will to stamp out drugs or are afraid that the cost in civil liberties will be too high. For whatever reason, a significant portion of the population does not want to go all out to save our children.

I take the opposite view. I believe that if we have been endowed by our Creator with certain inalienable rights, then someone who sells a person an addictive, life-destroying substance diminishes all of us. I do not believe that a drug addict passively waiting for the next fix is capable of being a free citizen. I do not believe an America that accepts widespread drug use is going to retain the spirit of optimistic individualism that has been our hallmark. Massive drug use may be acceptable in a more passive society, but it is antithetical to a free nation of self-reliant individuals.

Every time I get into a debate on this issue, the supporters of legalized drugs eventually concede that they would still want to ban certain drugs that induce violent behavior and would still want to prevent drugs from being sold to children. But then we would still have an illegal drug trade and would be back where we started.

The epidemic of poverty, dysfunction, and violence brought on by the drug trade is so much a threat to our children and our society that I believe we should design a thorough effort to destroy it. What I am about to outline would almost certainly lead to a dramatic decline of drug availability in America. It would also require decisive changes in how we deal with destructive people in our midst. My only defense is that it is a strategy that has worked historically. If you are not prepared to win the war on drugs, you must be prepared to accept the argument that accepts and legalizes drugs. When I look at my daughters and their husbands, my nieces and nephews, I know I am willing to go a long way to protect them. I have had personal experience with drug addiction among family members, students, and friends. The human cost is far too great for us to continue a half-hearted, defeatist approach.

There are countries around the world that have remarkably little drug use. They have achieved this through very strong cultural biases against using drugs and ruthless actions against those who sell drugs. There is no question that such a firm, no-nonsense approach could work in America.

First, we should have no sympathy for addicts and every sympathy for recovering addicts. We should work with every recovery program to develop low-cost detoxification programs. Our goal should be to have a twenty-four-hour, seven-day-a-week program where there is always a bed and a friend waiting if you are willing to kick your habit. There are more than enough churches, synagogues, and mosques in America to provide volunteers and facilities.

Second, as part of our carrot-and-stick approach, we should cut off any government funding that helps maintain drug addiction. Our goal should be to send every financial, psychological, and cultural signal that we refuse to subsidize people in dependency.

Third, the "Just Say No" campaign should be reinvigorated. Nancy Reagan *did* send a clear and compelling message to young people. The Coalition for a Drug-Free America has found that young people *do* respond to antidrug messages. Unfortunately, over the last three years the subtly permissive attitudes of the Clinton administration have sent out the wrong message, and drug use, after having declined, has started up again. Children can intuit when adults are serious and when they are simply paying lip service. Once again, we need to intensify the message that just saying no is morally and socially correct.

Fourth, drug users should face serious economic penalties. I would favor charging a user 10 percent of their gross assets for first conviction, 20 percent for second conviction, and 30 percent for third conviction. The first time a baseball player or rock star had to pay a multimillion-dollar fine, drugs would begin to lose their glamour. For public personalities, part of the penalty should also include spending one day a week at a rehabilitation program. People should feel financial and personal inconvenience for having violated the law.

Because our penalties seem so trivial to the wealthy, they have treated our drug laws with contempt. Every wealthy drug user is subsidizing a system that wreaks its violence and brutality on poorer people. They are accomplices in the drug trade. I have much more tolerance for a poor person who turns to drugs out of despair than for a successful person who turns to drugs out of boredom. Their self-indulgence subsidizes a system that is crippling our country, endangering our children, and killing our fellow citizens.

Fifth, domestic drug dealers should face sentences and confiscation of property that are as steep as the Constitution allows. If you are a drug dealer, all of your assets must be presumed to come from the drug trade unless proved otherwise. To the degree that we can't impoverish drug dealers, we should extend their sentences so they can't spend their money. There are no innocent drug dealers. Every dealer is part of a network of addiction, violence, and death. This message should be particularly communicated to people who presume that selling drugs is just a lark. They must have adequate warning that their behavior will not be tolerated. Every system of communication utilized by potential drug dealers ought to be filled with announcements about the new penalties and attitudes.

Sixth, anyone importing commercial quantities of drugs

should be regarded as an invader of our national boundaries. The drug assault on our borders has produced more casualties among the young, the innocent, and the weak than all but our biggest wars. We should regard this as an act of war against our people. The response should be the same as against any military invader. I strongly favor a mandatory death penalty for entering our territory with a commercial quantity of illegal drugs.

Seventh, we should intensify our intelligence efforts against drug lords across the planet and help foreign governments to trap them. We should track their money and interdict it wherever possible. We should also use whatever means necessary to destroy their operations and impoverish their personal accounts. In effect, we should say, "Close down your operations or expect the full weight of the United States to be used against you on every front." The wiser drug lords will leave the trade and keep their current fortunes.

The Royal Navy spent the first third of the nineteenth century interdicting the slave trade in a determined effort to wipe it out. Their unilateral efforts increased the risks and gradually abolished the practice. We should take a similarly aggressive stance against the slavery of drug addiction.

This seven-step program would radically reduce violence and drug dependency in America. For our children's sake, it is the right direction, the right scale, and the right intensity.

CHAPTER 19

Defense for the Twenty-first Century: Reflections of a Cheap Hawk

The United States today has the most professional and most advanced peacetime military in our history. The forces who executed Desert Shield and Desert Storm represented a level of training, doctrine, and investment in new equipment that was literally a generation ahead of the Iraqi forces they opposed. The results showed in the war. There had not been such a one-sided victory since the Anglo-Egyptian forces defeated the Mahdi's medieval army at Omdurman in the Sudan in 1898.

Yet the United States can no more rest on its laurels than the British could. Immediately after Omdurman the British found themselves mired down in the Boer War in South Africa. They ultimately won it with enormous effort. Eleven years later the British found themselves up against a large, modern German opponent and suffered horrendous casualties in Flanders Fields at the beginning of World War I.

We must recognize that any number of clever countries with professional militaries are studying our victories and trying to learn how to cope with an American military force. Some of them have large armies (Russia, India, China), some have advanced technologies, and a few seem willing to take very high risks through terrorism and other techniques (Libya, Iran, Iraq, North Korea). We have to plan based on the assumption that somewhere there may be an opponent with the courage and determination to test us in circumstances that we have not considered, using systems that we have not invented ourselves. Complacency is the father of defeat. Vigilance is the mother of continued safety.

In 1981 I helped found the Military Reform Caucus, along with Sam Nunn, Gary Hart, Paul Trible, Bill Whitehurst, and Dick Cheney. During the 1980s we urged the Pentagon to think more aggressively about new doctrine and new approaches to equipment, procurement, and organization.

I am a hawk but a cheap hawk. I don't think we ought to salute waste just because it is in uniform. I also don't think the Pentagon should be any more exempt from reengineering, downsizing, and rethinking than any other part of the federal government.

Conservatives have a particular responsibility in thinking about reorganizing the Pentagon. We complained for a generation about McNamara's bureaucracy and its unnecessary layers of civilian micromanagement. Now is the time to flatten the organizational chart and decentralize minor decision making. Our goal should be to downsize the Pentagon until it seems to be at most a triangle.

We should seek to reduce the time it takes to develop new weapons to 20 percent of the currently absurd, multiyear process. The P–51 Mustang was designed and flown in four months. The B–52 was redesigned over one weekend in a hotel in Dayton after the air force told Boeing it did not like the original design. The contract for the B–47 (which Boeing located and gave me) is about seventy pages. In contrast, the paperwork for the C–5a is so bulky it would take five C–5a's (our military's largest transport) to carry it.

We should adopt a multiyear acquisition process for major weapons. All of the management innovations of Deming and Peter Drucker, combined with all of the advantages of quality, just-in-time inventories, and reengineering are useless when Congress goes through a series of start/stop procurement orders. Every time a major contractor renegotiates a contract with their subcontractors, the paperwork costs $30 million. The process is repeated three or four times a year because of congressional uncertainty about funding. This wasted $100 million becomes overhead and is regularly cited by liberals as proof that new weapons cost too much.

If we bought a three-year contract and debated renewal of the third year on an annual basis, we could smooth the noise out of the system and allow modern management to work. The third-year renewal is something a lot of football coaches use. If it will save us billions, it is worth pursuing. One major contractor said that it could deliver at 40 percent less cost if it could just get stable funding and concentrate on production.

These kinds of reforms in management bureaucracy and procurement systems would save us a great deal of money. They would also provide a better defense with more modern equipment at lower cost. It is important to remember that the ultimate purpose of reforming the Pentagon is not merely to save money. The real purpose is to force a process of systematic reform that will enable us to defend America and our allies better and with lower risks.

While I am a cheap hawk, I remain a hawk. I believe the world is a dangerous place. I believe there are active enemies who would love to destroy the United States. I believe our opponents are clever and determined and deserve our respect. I believe we need to have a much bigger investment in intelligence and make a much bigger effort to stop terrorism. When in doubt, I favor a stronger rather than a weaker America. If you compare the Korean War with Desert Storm, you can understand my passion. North Korea gambled that America was weak and would not act. When we did respond, our forces were undertrained, underequipped, and too small. In the first months of the Korean War, a lot of Americans and South Koreans died unnecessarily because we had not maintained our strength. Desert Storm was exactly the opposite. A strong America won decisively with minimum losses to our young and our allies. The decisive difference was the Reagan military buildup of the 1980s as compared with the Truman defense demobilization of the late 1940s.

Since Desert Storm, liberals have been consistently reducing our military strength. We would have a hard time achieving the decisive success of Desert Storm today. If we continue to under-invest in equipment and training, we will once again be putting our young men and women at risk.

The best of the professional military understand that their world and ours is changing. They know that the revolution in information systems is going to create a revolution in warfare. They know that the collapse of the Soviet Union has actually widened our range of responsibilities and is spreading our forces even thinner across the planet. They know that the proliferation of weapons of mass destruction—nuclear, biological, and chemical—is going to make the risks vastly greater. They know that the rise of international terrorism and the fanaticism of Islamic fundamentalists creates new risks and new problems that we have not successfully solved.

Our uniformed military is now challenged on several fronts. They must deal simultaneously with specific crises wherever and whenever they emerge, respond to the need for reduced military manpower, consult constantly with our allies. At the same time, they must think through the emerging nature of this new world and the even more dramatic emerging nature of the Third Wave Information Revolution. Finally, they must be able to educate the elected leadership, the news media, and interested citizens so the correct policies and institutions can be sustained.

The challenge to our generation is enormous. No country has ever had the potential to lead the entire human race the way America does today. No country has ever had as many people of as many different backgrounds call on it as we do today. No country has ever had as many neighbors who suspect, distrust, and, in some cases, hate one another call on it to help achieve peace and help transform conflict into community. No country has ever had as many former dictatorships call on it for advice about how to create free government, free markets, and a military that can operate within the rule of law and under civilian control.

The simple fact is that with the end of the Cold War and the collapse of the Soviet empire, the need for American leadership has become greater. With the decentralization of power away from Moscow and the dramatic explosion of communications, markets, and weapons inherent in the Third Wave Information Age, the burden on America has grown greater. Our generation must rise to the challenge or our children will live in a violent and war-torn world.

The Romans had a simple rule: if you want peace, prepare for war. George Washington echoed the same theme as the result of his lifetime struggle for the cause of freedom. Peace through strength will work. Peace through weakness is impossible. Frugal yes, foolish no—those should be our watchwords.

CHAPTER 20

New Frontiers in Science, Space, and the Oceans

I am amazed every time I hear reports of teen suicide or stories about people who despair because of boredom or because they have nothing left to look forward to. We are on the verge of enormous frontiers of knowledge and opportunity, although our elite and entertainment cultures are so negative and cynical (and so scientifically and technologically ignorant) that you would never know it. They fail to energize the sense of excitement that is potentially available to all of us.

From exploring space to plumbing the oceans' depths to discoveries of molecular medicine to the unexplored worlds of computers and virtual reality, we are on the threshold of great achievements. Our lives are going to be enriched and expanded by inventions and discoveries of which we now have only the vaguest ideas.

Our generation is still seeking its Jules Verne or H. G. Wells to dazzle our imaginations with hope and optimism. Instead we have writers like Michael Crichton, whose work is just standard alarmist environmentalism in which humans are forever messing up nature, a Frankenstein story in which curious scientists are the villains.

Why not aspire to build a real Jurassic Park? (It may not be at all impossible, you know.) Wouldn't that be one of the most spectacular accomplishments of human history? What if we could bring back extinct species? Why not take Crichton's negative vision a few steps further and actually celebrate the awesome potential of our future?

Arthur C. Clarke is a science fiction writer who truly embraces the future. No wonder it was Clarke who in 1948 proposed the system of communications satellites that today links our long-distance and cellular phones and enables us to call around the world. His positive vision actually stimulated discoveries.

Somehow we must reintegrate the scientific with the popular and reconnect the future to the present. This is less a job for scientists, engineers, bureaucrats, and administrators and more a job for novelists, moviemakers, popularizers, and politicians.

I am deeply committed to expanding the awareness of the science and engineering that will make the future more dynamic. I believe in the extraordinary potential of human beings to work together in creating more opportunities for everyone. As long as we have hope, we have the ability to pull together as a team to achieve a better future.

If young people were to learn from school and the media that the future could be better—if more teachers were to become infected with the idea that the twenty-first century will be a century of opportunity—there would be a remarkably different mood in America. Studying makes sense when you are preparing for a great adventure. A generation that learns its magic from Tom Swift or Jules Verne has a much more optimistic outlook than one that is constantly being told that the planet is dying and that everything humanity is doing is wrong. When I was young, Frank Buck's Bring-'em-Back-Alive adventures, Lindbergh's solo flight across the Atlantic, Arthur C. Clarke's visions of space exploration, and the American Museum's diving bell exploring the deep oceans made me believe there was a whole universe waiting to be learned and explored. Life was truly a grand adventure.

Now, at fifty-one years of age, I am still convinced that this positive vision of my childhood was the right one. But somehow our culture has lost its way. I believe more than ever that much remains to be discovered and that many great adventures remain to be launched. Life in the twenty-first century will mean opening up the oceans around us, pushing out into the solar system, mapping the human gene, exploring worlds of data and information that we have only just begun to understand.

One of the major reasons the spirit of adventure has gone out of space exploration is that we have allowed bureaucracies to dominate too many of our scientific adventures. Look at the difference between the movies *The Right Stuff* and *Star Wars* and you will see what I mean. Bureaucracies are designed to minimize risk and to create orderly systematic procedures. In a way they tend to be inherently dull. They also tend to be slow, cumbersome, and expensive. Imagine what the Lewis and Clark expedition would have been if it had been run by today's government. Instead of a small, dedicated, and courageous band launching into the unknown and reaching the Pacific Ocean, there would have been a large cumbersome, slow-moving, and cautious committee of researchers who would have been lucky to reach the Rocky Mountains.

I recently asked an aerospace executive what would happen if we got the government out of the business of designing space shuttles and space stations. She replied that the cost would drop by 40 percent and the amount of time would be cut in half. Then I asked a senior designer for another aerospace company how we could best buy a second-generation shuttle. He replied that a space shuttle was technically about as complicated as a commercial airliner and should cost as much. Thus the next-generation space shuttle, which is currently estimated at $36 billion, really should be built for about $10 billion. To his credit, Dan Golden, the current head of NASA, understands these principles and is doing everything he can to turn them into reality. With his help we are going to create a more exciting future in space.

Jerry Pournelle, an aerospace engineer and science fiction writer, notes that going into orbit takes about the same amount of energy as traveling from Los Angeles to Sydney, Australia. In principle, a ticket to go into orbit should not be dramatically more expensive than a first class ticket to Australia.

I believe that space tourism will be a common fact of life during the adulthood of children born this year, that honeymoons in space will be the vogue by 2020. Imagine weightlessness and its effects and you will understand some of the attractions. Imagine looking out at the Earth from your honeymoon suite and you will understand even more why it will be a big item. For those who have everything, a long trip in space will be the equivalent of today's sailboat or yacht or private airplane.

The challenge for us is to get government and bureaucracy out of the way and put scientists, engineers, entrepreneurs, and adventurers back into the business of exploration and discovery. The twenty-first century should be as great a century of exploration for humanity as the sixteenth was for the Europeans. Now that is an exciting future.

The next time people tell you they are bored, ask if they have thought about any of these opportunities. See if you can get them to join us on the great adventures of the twenty-first century.

CHAPTER 21

Tending the Gardens of the Earth: Scientifically Based Environmentalism

My interest in the environment goes back to my childhood. For some reason, I was fascinated by animals and nature long before I went to school. My early professional dreams were of becoming a zoo director or a vertebrate paleontologist (I have a Tyrannosaurus rex skull in the Speaker's office). I loved stories about collecting wild animals and fossils. Whenever I could I would talk my relatives into visiting zoos and museums.

I also collected animals, although my mom and dad would routinely make me release them. My mother had a particular aversion to snakes, which of course meant they interested me a lot. I finally resolved this problem in adulthood when my wife agreed I could have any snake I wanted as long as it was in ZooAtlanta. Marianne promptly gave them two emerald tree boas, which have since been followed by two rhinoceroses and two Komodo dragons. All are now at ZooAtlanta.

At a fairly early age, I began reading about the extinctions humans had caused around the planet. The loss of the dodo was one. Killing off the giant moa of New Zealand struck me as a particular tragedy, and the loss of the Carolina parakeet, whose numbers once darkened the sky for days, seemed incomprehensible to me.

My political orientation as a Republican reinforced this sense of conservation and the awareness that man has the potential to do terrible damage. The conservation movement was begun by Republicans. Gifford Pinchot, who personified the fight for national forests, was the progressive ally of Theodore Roosevelt. It was President Taft's firing of Pinchot that led to the split of the Republican Party and Theodore Roosevelt's Bull Moose campaign in 1912.

I read about William Hornaday, founder of the New York Zoological Society, who helped save the American bison—one of the first successful conservation efforts. Studying these events helped me understand the efforts made to save the natural world from man's depredations.

During my first year of teaching, I participated in the first Earth Day. In a short time, I found myself the coordinator of environmental studies at West Georgia College. This was an interdisciplinary program that included biologists, physicists, geographers, and other interested faculty. For several years, we took students on field trips to the Okeefenokee Swamp, Cumberland Island on the Georgia coast, and the North Georgia Mountains. I introduced students to the concept of ecosystems, the role of man in nature, and the challenges our generation faces in preserving a livable planet for our descendants. It was one of my most enjoyable faculty experiences.

When I began to run for public office, I also worked with the Georgia Conservancy, the local Sierra Club chapter, the League of Conservation Voters, and other environmental groups. I found most of the volunteers eager and enthusiastic—even if their emotions did sometimes outrun their facts. After I was elected to Congress, I found that national environmental organizations were all too often simply an extension of the left wing of the Democratic Party. They wanted to defeat Republicans and elect Democrats, no matter what the substance of the issues. It was a very trying time. The more I worked with Presidents Reagan and Bush, the harder it was to find common ground with the Sierra Club and the League of Conservation Voters. Still, I have retained, and indeed expanded, my original vision of an economically rational, scientifically based environmentalism.

After twenty-five years of experience, we are now at a point where we can look back at our effort, review what worked and what failed, and try to establish a powerful foundation for a new era of environmental success.

For me, any such effort begins with the premise that man dominates the planet and that we have an absolute obligation to minimize damage to the natural world. I am not a preservationist. It is impossible for us to be a dynamic species and still act as if we don't exist. We can't help having an impact on the environment. We should also recognize that there are a lot of natural rhythms (including weather and geologic rhythms of which we may not be aware) that guarantee the planet will be changing all the time. We should try to conserve along with this dynamic environment instead of trying to stop all change.

In Rene Dubos's term, we have to become gardeners of the Earth. As the book of Genesis says, we have an obligation to cultivate that which God has given us. Gardeners are not looters and despoilers. Neither are they Eastern holy men who refuse to kill any living thing, even if it is endangering them.

We have three basic motivations: aesthetics, public health, and new knowledge. Aesthetically, our lives are much richer if we cultivate and maintain the Earth's diversity. A planet with elephants, blue whales, and a wide variety of birds and butterflies, plus natural beauties such as Yellowstone Park and the Grand

Canyon, is far more desirable than one that is covered with parking lots and high-rise apartments. Our quality of life will be much better if we maintain wilderness areas, national parks, nature preserves, migratory bird paths, and similar facilities.

Getting back in touch with nature is an intrinsic pleasure we all share. We have only been an urban animal for a few thousand years. As most New Yorkers can attest, Central Park makes Manhattan an infinitely more enjoyable place. I live only three miles northwest of the Chattahoochee River National Recreation Center and seven miles southeast of the Kennesaw Mountain Civil War Battlefield Park. I walk in both areas whenever I can and my outlook on life invariably improves.

Public health is another major reason for tending the environment. Bad air was a major health problem in London, New York, and Los Angeles (but has improved in all three). Toxic-waste dumps, mercury pollution, and DDT poisoning are only a few of the ways in which the public health is affected by carelessly destructive behavior. Anyone who doubts that environmental pollution can be a public health menace should visit Mexico City or any part of the former Soviet empire. The latter is also vivid proof that government-controlled economies are much worse for the environment than free-market ones.

Our third reason for caring about our environment is derived from the power of knowledge. If we agree that human beings have a moral obligation to take care of the ecosystem, then we need to gather scientific data and make rational assessments of the costs. It is foolish to think we can spend unlimited resources solving every environmental problem. If nothing else, the funds squandered on one problem will be unavailable for others. To get the best ecosystem for our buck, we should use decentralized and entrepreneurial strategies rather than command-and-control bureaucratic efforts.

This was brought home to me about five years ago when the people who make telephone poles came to see me. They were facing a regulatory ruling that would have destroyed their entire industry. The government was going to require a change in chemical treatments even though it would be radically more difficult and more expensive. There would be virtually no public-health gain. The Office of Management and Budget did a cost-benefit analysis and discovered that the program would spend seven trillion dollars for each life saved. The misallocation of resources was so grotesque that even the OMB rejected it.

New studies indicate that the asbestos program probably wasted $5 billion without significantly improving public health. That would have been enough money to map most of the world's ecosystems. The Superfund program spent nearly 40 percent of its billions on lawyers and bureaucrats. Only one-fifth went to cleaning up waste sites. That money could have saved a lot of endangered species.

Many environmental regulations hatched in Washington put a ridiculous burden on small communities. Rules and regulations that make sense for a big city can bankrupt a small town. Again and again these communities complain of the rigid attitudes in Washington—and in the EPA's regional offices, which are much worse.

Misdesigned programs, questionable science, and rigid bureaucratic enforcement have caused a loss of momentum to our environmental effort. If the current slowdown is seen as an opportunity to reassess and rethink, it will be a good thing. If it becomes an excuse for developers and businesses to undermine a sound environmentalism, it will be a bad thing. The American public will not allow us to turn back on the environment.

Yet we need more knowledge of the natural world for deeper reasons than merely saving the environment. As we enter the age of molecular medicine, we may discover thousands of cures and drugs from organisms that we have not yet even identified. As we learn more about ourselves as organic beings, we are discovering more and more about the natural world that relates to how we function and what our needs are. We need to know more about the environment so that we can know more about ourselves.

One starting point should be to develop a worldwide biological inventory. The simple fact is, we don't know enough about the animal and plant life on the planet. The amount we currently spend on learning about the natural world is surprisingly small. If we could agree on creating this inventory, it could establish a knowledge base that would be the foundation for a broad range of advances in human and environmental health and in our understanding of the world we live in and the way we live in it.

A second step would be to identify endangered habitats as well as endangered species and to look for practical solutions. The Endangered Species Act is often used to impose a level of regulatory interference that is not sustainable in a free society. When people are cutting down bushes and trees on their properties—as they are now doing in the West—for fear that endangered species will be attracted there, we know we are doing something wrong. Their fear is that the government will take functional control of their lands and thus having an endangered species visit becomes a frightening rather than enjoyable event. Clearly that is no way to run a free society.

It may be possible to find ways of preserving endangered species through enhanced breeding rather than simply blocking all change in the environment. All too often the legitimate environmental viewpoint is crowded out by a noisy preservationism that has no scientific basis but simply condemns all human presence in the environment.

We also need hardheaded management with regard to costs and benefits. If a billion dollars spent one way will save one species and the same amount spent in a different way will save thirty species, we should opt for the more efficient investment of our resources. We could have done so much more to maintain such a diversity of species with a fraction of the money wasted on Superfund. Part of such a commonsense approach might be to allow more flexibility at home while spending more on preservation efforts abroad.

By encouraging pro-environmental technologies, we can

achieve bigger breakthroughs than we can get through clumsy retrofitting and cleanup-type approaches. Congressman Bob Walker is pushing a hydrogen-fuel initiative that might produce less pollution at lower cost and limit our dependence on foreign fuels. Several oil companies have proposed establishing a trust fund in Los Angeles that would help retire heavily polluting pre–1980 cars by replacing them with newer models. The program would achieve six times the reduction in air pollution as an equally expensive set of oil-refinery regulations being pushed by the EPA. A similar innovation in the electrical generating industry—a system of tradable air-pollution permits—has produced cleaner air for one-third the anticipated costs. Wherever we can, we should adopt decentralized, market-oriented approaches. We will get much better results than are possible with the red-tape-ridden, bureaucratically controlled system in place today.

We should emphasize recycling wherever it makes sense. Shaw Industries, in Georgia, which has 38 percent of the U.S. carpet market, is developing a recycling program that will revolutionize the industry. Carpets make up 4 percent of all solid waste. Under the plan, municipal dumps will pay Shaw to take away their carpet remains. Landfill space will be saved and Shaw will recycle the material into new carpets, saving resources in the process.

I have a constituent in my district, Linda Bavaro, who was bored after her children went to school. "You can only shop so long," she told me. She had been a marketing major in college, and she began looking for something to do. Recycling seemed economically and psychologically satisfying. Researching at her local library, she discovered a firm in North Carolina that was doing research on how to turn the two-liter Coke bottle into clothing fibers. She drove to North Carolina and saw for herself that it worked. Next, she got a contract with Coca-Cola to recycle old bottles. Then she got a commitment from Disney World to sell her T-shirts. Today she has a successful company, Global Green, as a result of environmental concern, entrepreneurial courage, and a commitment to lifetime learning. Linda has a good chance of doing well financially by doing good environmentally. That is how a healthy free market in a free country ought to work.

From serious scientific surveys to new technologies, from recycling to commonsense management of ecosystems, we have the opportunity to launch a new era of environmentalism. We can craft an approach that is scientifically sound, economically rational, and politically popular. That is a worthy goal for the twenty-first century.

CHAPTER 22

Violent Crime, Freedom from Fear, and the Right to Bear Arms

Whenever I am asked about violent crime and the right to bear arms, I feel that I have to back up to first principles and explore the questioner's assumptions. The liberal bias and misinformation on these topics have been particularly relentless and consistently wrongheaded.

The persistently skewed condition of this debate was driven home to me at my first State of the Union address as Speaker of the House. Sitting behind the President of the United States for the first time as he spoke to the nation, I was well aware that I represented the institution of the House and had an obligation to represent the solemnity of the occasion on behalf of all my colleagues. But there was one moment when I almost forgot my resolve: When President Clinton explained that he was a duck hunter and described the weaponry that sport requires.

In the midst of that serious occasion, I wondered, Does he think the Second Amendment protects the right to hunt ducks? Honestly, I was astonished that his staff had allowed that comment into a serious national address like the State of the Union.

With that single line the President proved to everyone who cares about the Second Amendment that he did not have a clue about what concerns them. The Second Amendment to the Constitution has nothing to do with deer or duck hunting. It has nothing to do with target practice or owning collector's weapons. The Second Amendment is a political right written into our Constitution for the purpose of protecting individual citizens from their own government. The lesson of the English Civil War and the American Revolution was that political freedom is ultimately based on the courage and preparedness of those who would remain free. If the Lexington and Concord minutemen had not kept weapons, they could not have fired the shot heard 'round the world. If the American colonists had not been trained in how to shoot and fight, they could not have become American citizens.

The history of the last quarter-century has been a brutal reminder of the wisdom of the Founding Fathers. Poland and Hungary were disarmed, and when their citizens tried to rebel, they had no weapons with which to defend their country or their freedom. Afghanistan was an intensely armed country, on the other hand, and the Soviets found it impossible to break their spirit of freedom. Those who believe in the right to bear arms felt more than vindicated by the remarkably different results in the struggle for freedom between armed and unarmed populations.

Generally, liberals neither understand nor believe in the constitutional right to bear arms. Instead, they offer two extremely misleading arguments that frankly work well in isolating and ridiculing those who stand with the Founding Fathers in defending freedom.

First, the liberals associate guns with violence and argue that to be antiviolence is to be antigun. Second, they take the most extreme view of the right to bear arms, distort it, and then argue that only unreasonable people would fail to compromise in the name of "common sense."

My response on this issue is really quite simple. Our problem is not with weapons but with criminals; we should be concerned not with legislating against weaponry but with legislating against crime.

The simple equation of guns equal violent crime simply doesn't add up. For example, consider the most famous trial in America today. The O. J. Simpson case involves the alleged killing of an ex-wife and her friend by someone who used a sharp instrument. There was no gun involved.

Consider the most famous case of violence and murder in the 1988 presidential campaign. Willy Horton killed a young man by stabbing him more than a dozen times with a knife and then dumping his body in a fifty-gallon drum. When he got out of jail, Horton kidnapped a young woman and her fiancé and used a knife to torture him and rape her. Horton didn't seem to think guns were necessary to his violent behavior.

I recently participated in a press conference with a young woman from Columbus, Ohio, who was the victim of a serial rapist released from prison after several previous convictions. Working out in the prison weight room, he had built up such strength that he did not need to use weapons anymore. She is bitterly opposed to access to weight rooms for dangerous and violent people. I have held the same position ever since this particular absurdity was pointed out to me by a federal prison guard at one of my town-hall meetings.

Try talking to an antigun liberal about prison weight rooms and you will be told, "But they've got to be kept busy somehow." For some psychological reason, liberals are antigun but not anti–violent criminal. In fact, for all its hyperbole about gun control, the Clinton administration has still refused to charge convicted felons with the additional ten-year penalty they could get for using firearms in the commission of a felony. The administration is none too eager to go after law-breakers but is determined to harass law-abiding, middle-class citizens.

The second half of the liberal argument, the need to ban certain types of "dangerous" weapons, makes a great emotional argument. Factually, it is nonsense. In the first place, truly automatic weapons have been illegal since 1934. The most dangerous guns in America are not pseudo–assault weapons but pistols. The pseudo–assault weapons that liberals regularly try to ban are extraordinarily rare. Some are picked for the most childish reasons (their plastic stocks "looked militaristic"). One New Jersey police chief commented that a policeman is more likely to face a tiger escaped from a traveling circus than a weapon on the liberals' list.

Refuting the liberal strategy is quite easy. Washington and New York have the most stringent gun-control laws in the nation. In both cities every crime committed with a gun is already illegal. In almost every case, the very possession of the gun is already illegal. If gun control worked, shouldn't New York and Washington be quiet, peaceful cities? The tragedy that struck Jim Brady was committed by an assassin with a concealed illegal handgun, not a pseudo–assault weapon. No matter what weapon the assassin was carrying, he was already violating the law. Once again, Washington's so-called stringent gun control proved to be totally ineffective.

If gun control is not the answer, what should we do to make America safer and free us from fear? First, we can recognize the constitutional provision for a "well ordered militia" and decree that the mentally ill and convicted felons do not meet the test of being well ordered. Therefore, the first step should be to accelerate the instant identity-check system that would compare a thumbprint against a national record of felons and people who have been in mental institutions. No law-abiding citizen's thumbprint would be kept, but the lawbreaker and the insane would be picked up immediately if they tried to buy a gun.

The second step would be to make it illegal for convicted felons to carry guns under any circumstances unless they had received pardons. I am prepared to support a lifetime penalty for possession of a firearm if that is what it takes to separate violent criminals from their guns. If convicted felons knew that by carrying a gun they would go to prison for life by being stopped for speeding or jaywalking, they would be a lot more cautious about being armed.

The third step is to establish that prisoners should work forty-eight hours a week and study twelve hours a week. Numerous people in poor neighborhoods say that the young men in their areas refer to prison as "vacation time." They eat better, bulk up, and—as one woman in Atlanta put it—"come out looking sleek as seals." Prison in its current form is more an inconvenience than a deterrent.

The fourth step is to eliminate all weight and muscle-building rooms and break down the cult of macho behavior in prison. Prisoners should be learning job skills and doing penance. We must reclaim the prisons just as we must reclaim the streets.

The key is to focus our attention on violent people and not be drawn off into emotionally satisfying detours that harass the honest citizen but have no impact on crime.

Finally, we ought to teach in school once again why there is a Second Amendment and why the Founding Fathers thought the right to bear arms ought to be part of the Bill of Rights. After all, if the President of the United States thinks the Second Amendment is about duck hunting, we shouldn't be surprised if a lot of other citizens are confused, too.

If we deal effectively with criminals, we will have nothing to worry about from guns. In Switzerland, every adult male up to age forty-five is required to keep a semi-automatic rifle at home as part of the national defense system. Despite this extraordinary proliferation of guns, no one in Switzerland is anxiety-ridden. In Israel, it is common on weekends to see young people walking around Jerusalem or Tel Aviv with Uzis at their sides. They are on leave from the Israeli Defense Force and are required to carry their weapons. Far from making people feel insecure, the sight of the weapons makes people feel safer. It is not the gun but the purpose behind the gun that matters. It is not guns but violence that we must suppress. Any effort to divert our attention to a false trail actually increases the potential that the criminally violent will continue to prey on innocent Americans.

The recent tragedy in Oklahoma City is one more illustration of the liberal confusion between violence and guns. The tragedy is vivid in my memory. I visited Oklahoma City between four-thirty and six-thirty in the morning three days after the bombing. I deliberately went in when the news media would be asleep, and in those two hours I learned a lot. The sight of a nine-story building that had lost its entire front was even more horrible than the pictures on the news showed. The fluorescent arrows that pointed out where bodies were believed to be buried (but the building was too unsafe and unstable to get them out) were haunting. The exhaustion of the rescue workers who had been putting in over-twelve-hour days in a risky environment was evident at first glance and I tried to thank each of them personally for their commitment. The FBI coordination center was extremely impressive and the work of James Lee Witt and the Federal Emergency Management Agency was equally compelling.

When I got back to Atlanta, one reporter immediately asked me if the Oklahoma City bombing would lead to more restrictions on so-called assault weapons. I stared in disbelief. The building had been destroyed with a truck bomb made of fertilizer and fuel oil. The people who did it were murderers and it was irrelevant that the murder weapons were commercially available and could be put into a rental vehicle. It was the act of murder that was the crime and the focus had to be on catching and punishing the criminals.

Yet somehow the tragic killing of Americans was now going to be twisted by liberals in the news media into an attack on weapons that had not been used and on conservatives. It is precisely those who favor the right to bear arms who are prepared to support strong intelligence agencies and a strong national defense so that Americans can be protected from those who would kill them. It is very often those who favor banning guns who also favor banning the death penalty and who most often criticize our intelligence agencies and the very methods that are needed to stop the violence.

The Oklahoma City bombing and the news media's reaction to it reminded me once again of how emotional, how misguided, and how biased the coverage of violence and the coverage of the right to bear arms has become.

CHAPTER 23

Why Rush Limbaugh and His Friends Matter

When I first became active in politics, the overwhelming source of information was the elite media. The editorial writers and TV news commentators defined what the debate was about and how people were supposed to think. On the fringe of their overwhelming presence was a handful of interesting characters who had the audacity to differ. They were always on radio. When I first started teaching at West Georgia College in the early 1970s, Neil Boortz, in Atlanta, was one of those pioneers.

Gradually more and more people began to find talk radio interesting. Wes Minter built up a big audience on WSB (he is now in Minneapolis) and Bob Grant became famous in New York City on WABC.

The talk-radio world changed dramatically with the rise of Rush Limbaugh. Suddenly, millions of Americans were listening to a powerful advocate of their views. The news was being interpreted by someone whose values were much closer to the average American than were those of the elite media. The average

American began to enjoy listening to someone puncture the liberals' balloon and deflate the prestige of the editorialists and columnists.

Limbaugh's unique personality and style make him an extraordinary entertainer-commentator. His audience is vast. But what really caught the attention of the press was when his first book became a runaway bestseller. Suddenly he was challenging the print media in their home territory.

The talk-radio phenomenon goes much deeper than Limbaugh's biting remarks and humorous conversation. Michael Reagan brings his unique insights to a national network. Sean Hannity in Atlanta represents a new generation of young, attractive family-oriented talk-show hosts.

All across America there is a generation of new voices and new ideas. We did not realize how big the talk-show industry had become until we changed the House rules to allow them to broadcast from the Capitol. The television networks control the radio-TV gallery in the House and they ruled that talk-radio hosts were not reporters and could not use the press rooms.

When I became Speaker, we decided to sidestep a fight with the established media by simply giving the talk shows another space in the Capitol. Little did any of us realize what an outpouring of national and local shows would soon arrive. Nor were they just passive observers. Roger Hedgecock, the top-rated host in San Diego, brought a planeload of listeners who spent three days walking the corridors promoting the Contract with America while Roger broadcast from the basement of the Capitol.

By the end of the hundred days, the flood of radio hosts had become almost overwhelming. During the last week of the Contract, we had over forty talk shows broadcasting from the Capitol. Space was so short that we had shows broadcasting from the corridor outside my office and from the balcony outside my window. Every time my stomach growled, I felt it was being broadcast on national radio. The elite media still controlled the news gallery, but it seemed that the radio talk-show hosts had taken over the rest of the building.

All things considered, I like having talk shows in the Capitol because it brings an undisciplined, inquisitive back-home kind of curiosity to what's going on. Talk shows are not simply more conservative than the elite media; they are a lot less cynical. Talk-show hosts are usually pleased to have someone drop by and actually engage in interesting conversation. They may have a strong streak of skepticism, but they are not infected with the corrosive contempt and cynicism of the regular press corps.

One of the consistent characteristics of talk-show hosts is that they tend to have very strong personalities. They are classic examples of good, old-fashioned American individualism. After all, if you are going to put yourself on the line day after day, letting your audience raise any question and argue about any opinion, you are probably a pretty self-confident person. If you are willing to live and die by the ratings, you are obviously a risk-taker.

Talk shows have done three big things for the country. First, they give people a place to ventilate and have a public dialogue rather than simply being lectured to by the elite commentators. Second, they have created a unifying sense of confidence among millions of listeners that it is okay to be conservative and challenge the liberal wisdom. Third, when the elite media have tried to distort the news, the talk shows have a pretty good record of setting things straight over the following four or five days.

I would not want to live in an America where the only source of information was talk radio. But as long as the elite media remains so cynical and so out of touch with average Americans, I sure am glad we have Rush Limbaugh and his friends to keep us company, keep us informed, and keep us on the offense.

CHAPTER 24

The Flat Tax and the IRS

A taxpayers' rebellion is brewing in America. It is going to force us either to adopt a flat tax or to replace the entire income tax system with a consumption tax. I would not have written those words five months ago. I knew there were a lot of people who were tired of the current income tax system. I knew that Congressman Dick Armey had a fascinating proposal for a flat tax that could be filed on a postcard. But frankly I did not see the explosion of desire for change building among the American people.

Dick Armey had been telling me that he was getting a tremendous reaction from across the country. Bill Archer, the new chairman of the Ways and Means Committee, had already indicated that he wanted to start hearings during the summer of 1995 to explore bold changes in the income tax system. I had noted both reports but they had not made any impression on me.

Then, on the third Saturday in January, I attended a town-hall meeting that was a wakeup call for me. I had established a system of teaching my course, Renewing American Civilization, every Saturday at Reinhardt College. From there I went to different parts of my district for a town-hall meeting in the afternoon. Our goal was to stay in touch with the grassroots attitudes during the first phase of implementing the Contract with America.

For two hours on this particular Saturday we had been listening to standard comments about the Contract and the Congress. Then I recognized a woman who I thought would be our last speaker for the day. Boy, was I wrong!

She announced that she was a tax attorney. "I earn a living helping my clients find ways not to pay their taxes," she began. "The system is so complex that I am able to find a lot of loopholes, but frankly the process is now so sick that I would like you to eliminate the whole system. I will make a living as a cabinet-maker or something, but I sure don't need to keep making money out of helping people use an unfair tax code to avoid paying their fair share."

To my surprise, the reaction from the nearly six hundred people still there after two hours was overwhelming. I began to ask questions.

"How many of you would pay one hundred dollars a year more in taxes just to get a simple system?" I asked.

Every hand went up. Then a voice yelled from the back of the room, "How about two hundred and fifty dollars?"

I asked again. One-third of the hands went up.

"How many agree that there needs to be deep fundamental change in the system?" I went on.

All but two hands went up.

"How many oppose deep change?"

The two hands went up. "Those are the CPAs of the group," one man yelled.

They were.

I began asking similar questions week after week. The common thread seems to be a resentment at the ever-growing complexity of the tax code and its record keeping requirements combined with a sense of rage at the Internal Revenue Service's attitude. The tax code frightens people because they are never truly sure if they have done what they are supposed to do. It now requires a sophisticated level of knowledge just to do the paperwork in order to have your *accountant* do your taxes. Only the very wealthy can afford bookkeepers to turn records over to the accountant—and of course the wealthy are now so put off by the liberal Democrats' class-warfare attitudes that they are angry about what they pay even if they are less bothered by the paperwork.

Middle-class folks who resent the paperwork and the uncertainty find themselves enraged by the attitude of the IRS. My wife does our taxes. She says the IRS makes unreasonable demands, takes an unreasonable attitude, and has unreasonable power over individual citizens.

The recent announcement that the IRS is going to institute a lottery and start randomly auditing individual citizens created a further sense of anxiety and rage. One of the original Revolutionary War flags had a snake on it and the motto "Don't tread on me." It is easy to forget that at the heart of the American spirit remains an intense hostility to being coerced or intimidated.

Americans hardly rebelled against King George's taxation without representation in order to create our own tax inquisition. The increasing sense of the IRS as an intimidating force guarantees that the efforts to replace the current income tax system are going to be watched intensely.

I will not predict that either Dick Armey's flat tax or Bill Archer's consumption tax will be the winner. Senator Bob Dole and I have asked Jack Kemp to chair a commission of nine leading Americans to explore these and other ideas. They will report in October 1995. Their efforts, combined with the reaction to the hearings in the summer of 1995, will provide a good indication of what solution the American people want.

What I am certain of is that every day the IRS is increasing popular pressure for a bold, radical change. Overwhelmingly, this country will probably support some kind of reform of the income tax system. And that reform will come soon.

CHAPTER 25

The Coming Crisis
in Higher Education

As a former assistant professor at West Georgia College and
a Ph.D. in European History who recently taught at
Kennesaw State College, Reinhardt College, and the Industrial
College of the Armed Forces, I was fascinated to read in the
April 4, 1995, *New York Times* an article buried on page D24 that
is an early indicator of a crisis now looming in higher education.

Entitled "Professors Battling Television Technology," the
article reported on the surprise resignation of J. Michael
Orenduff, chancellor of the University of Maine. Orenduff, it
seems, had developed an "eighth campus" for the university,
which would be in effect a "virtual campus" that would exist only
electronically. Drawing on the latest in interactive television, the
campus would allow professors to lecture to thousands of students at interactive television sites around the state. Courses
would be piped in from as far away as South Carolina. It was a
brilliant effort, taking advantage of some of the latest developments in information technology.

The electronic campus was particularly suited to Maine. Although small in population, the state is large geographically, with a scattered rural population and hard winters. Taking courses by interactive television would be the perfect way for many Maine residents to avoid the hazards of winter driving. In short, Chancellor Orenduff probably deserved the gratitude of every Maine citizen.

On the other seven campuses, however, the professors didn't like it. The faculty—all members of the Associated Faculty of the University of Maine, an affiliate of the Maine Education Association—banded together to force Chancellor Orenduff's resignation. Orenduff's crime was that he was trying to offer the citizens of Maine more education for less money. The faculty— like any other guild or labor union—wanted to deliver less education for more money. Unfortunately, that is what the citizens of Maine are going to get.

For those who wonder about what is wrong with higher education, the *Times* article was a gold mine. "With shrinking budgets and increasing enrollments," said reporter William Honan, "many faculty members worry that universities will see distance learning and other technology as a way to lower the cost of education." Can you imagine anyone actually wanting to lower the cost of education? Can you imagine how bankrupt the American automobile companies would be today, for example, if they had accepted that rationale and avoided change?

"John Diamond, a spokesman for the university," Honan continued, "said the faculties were angry with Chancellor Orenduff's proposals to the State Legislature to consolidate the system by such means as having one dean serve two academic schools, publishing a common catalogue for all seven campuses, and conducting 'exit examinations' to determine how much students had learned."

Imagine a leader who actually wanted to lower costs, make information more convenient to customers, and insist on accountability for whether or not students were actually learning? Former Chancellor Orenduff ought to be a hero to taxpayers, parents, and students, but it is easy to understand why he is unacceptable to the faculty. Unfortunately, it was not the taxpayers, parents, or students but the faculty that had the last word.

This story is the tip of the iceberg. Put simply, higher education in this country is out of control. First, campuses are run for the benefit of the faculty, not the students. Second, tenured faculty have become increasingly out of touch with the rest of America, rejecting the culture of the people who pay their salaries. Third, there is an acceptance of higher costs without effective management by administrators. Take all three together and you can see that higher education and the general public are on a collision course.

College and university faculties have developed a game in which they have lots of petty power with very little accountability. The idea that the chancellor and trustees can be intimidated by the faculties is a comment on current social mythology rather than a realistic structure of power. There is no reason to assume that the current entrenched bureaucracies of higher learning have anyone's interests at heart but their own. There is no reason for the taxpayers, the trustees, or the students to think the faculties are protesting out of love of learning.

My dad was an ROTC officer at a state university in the early 1970s, and he was astonished at the viciousness and intensity of academic politics. Woodrow Wilson remarked eighty years earlier that after taking on the faculty senate as president of Princeton he found the United States Senate relatively easy to deal with. My experience on seven different campuses has been the same. A lot of what passes for academic debate is really maneuvering by departments for staff positions and resources. Precisely because so much of academic life is about small decisions, the fights become personal and petty.

We need a thorough review of higher education by outsiders to determine how America can best organize learning for adults. How can we offer the most effective and convenient education at the lowest cost? The results of such a study would be sobering to most faculty, but what other way do we have of moving these entrenched systems of privilege out of their enclaves of power?

Most tenured positions in higher education are now held by passionate advocates of the anti–Vietnam War movement. These former radicals have now become the comfortable, all-purpose "deconstructionists" of American culture. When I talk to older faculty members who still study such traditional figures as Jefferson, Franklin, and Washington, there is a sadness in their voices as they describe the atmosphere of intolerance and petty barbarism that has invaded American campuses.

Yale University recently had to return $20 million to oil tycoon Lee Bass because after several years the university could not get the faculty to agree to teach Western Civilization. Stephen Ambrose, a leading historian and author of *D-Day June 6, 1944*, noted recently in the *Wall Street Journal* (April 13, 1995) that on Thomas Jefferson's two hundred and fiftieth birthday not a single mention of his life was made at the Organization of American Historians. There were, however, seminars about radical history, labor history, gay and lesbian history, multicultural history, and all the other pet obsessions of contemporary academia. "As a consequence our children are being cheated," Ambrose concluded. "They have a legacy that comes from they know not where, paid for by men whose names they scarcely know (or, if they do know them, it is as slave-holders, imperialists, Daddy Warbucks, or Dr. Strangelove), at a price they cannot comprehend." Given this academic bias, is it any wonder American civilization and its values are not being transmitted to the next generation?

If the average taxpayer had a list of the ten weirdest courses their tax money was funding at their state university, they would ask for a refund. It's not just that their money is being wasted. It is being used to subsidize bizarre and destructive visions of reality. People are paying to have their own children miseducated.

Similarly, if every alumnus of private colleges and universities would insist on looking at their current catalogue before giving their next annual donation, there would be a rapid realignment in higher education. Most successful people get an annual letter saying, in effect, "Please give us money so we can hire someone who despises your occupation and will teach your children to have contempt for you." What is amazing is the overwhelming meekness of the alumni in accepting this hijacking of their alma mater.

All this would be laughable if it weren't destructive of America's future. First, ideas do have consequences. Having a generation brainwashed with a distorted version of reality is dangerous for our civilization. Second, the learning we are going to need if we are to compete in the world market is being obstructed by the pretensions of the academic elite.

Every American ought to have easy access to education through the most modern technologies. Every American ought to be able to learn the history and values of America. Every American ought to know about the competitiveness of the world market. Every American ought to be able to acquire occupational skills for a changing time. This means having access to a system of higher education that is responsive to the needs of the student rather than the concerns of the faculty.

College and university faculties are not Supreme Court justices. They are simply employees, and they should be subject to the same economic pressures as everyone else. When steelworkers are put out of jobs by changing technology, they can't go to the board of directors and insist they fire the chief executive officer who bought the new machinery. Yet that is exactly the way our universities are being run today.

When the public begins to assert its rights as consumers of education, rather than supplicants to an academic elite, we will begin to see rapid changes. American civilization will reemerge as an important concern of our educational system. Useful, functional learning will become accessible. The public will get its money's worth in knowledge and achievement.

Until we insist on these changes we should not be surprised to find ourselves being exploited. Every day that we wait, students are falsely educated, adult students find it unnecessarily difficult to upgrade their education, and public resources are wasted. The time to change higher education is now.

CHAPTER 26

Corrections Day

Corrections Day is a brand-new concept that is going to have a dramatic effect on the way government does business in Washington. Corrections Day will be held one day a month. On that day, the House will see that particularly destructive or absurdly expensive bureaucratic rules and regulations are overturned by narrowly drafted actions.

For my entire life, I've been listening to politicians explain to audiences that, although they can understand people's frustrations, they really have very little control over the bureaucracy. Again and again people go to their elected representative and bring some particularly harmful, arrogant, or wasteful behavior to their attention only to get sympathy—but no action.

This pattern has always bothered me because it undermines the legitimate power and authority of elected officials. After all, the Founding Fathers did not seek to replace King George's royal tyranny with an American bureaucratic tyranny. They thought they were creating a system in which free people could elect officials who were responsible for how things worked. Lincoln did not speak of "government by the bureaucrats, for the bureau-

223

crats, and of the bureaucrats." Any politician elected before 1960 would be astounded at the arrogance of institutions such as today's Environmental Protection Agency, Occupational Safety and Health Administration, and Fish and Wildlife Service. Bureaucratic arrogance goes hand in hand with congressional indifference. After all, Congress creates the bureaucracies. It appropriates the money and establishes the management systems that have gradually gotten out of control. If Congress wants to redesign the system, it obviously can.

What Congress is really saying when it allows the bureaucracy to run loose is that it believes the end will justify the means. Congress may not agree with some particular bureaucratic excess, but it still feels the goals are too important to overturn the system. In a democracy, however, the means are the end. No matter how clean or dirty our water may be, no matter how many industrial accidents we may or may not have, if we have to live in a society in which citizens constantly feel harassed, then the whole point of a free society is lost.

What are the possible solutions? Decentralizing power from Washington back to state and local government would obviously help. However, all too often the city, county, and state bureaucracies are worse than their federal counterparts.

Privatization of some government activities would probably also help. A monopoly has much less reason to be customer oriented than does a competitive system in which consumers have a choice. Just compare Federal Express and UPS with the U.S. Postal Service.

Unfortunately, the federal government is going to remain a large system for the foreseeable future. Even a remarkably small federal government would spend well over $1 trillion a year and have well over a million civilian employees. There are still things the people expect from the government. The public wants the federal government to play a strong role in protecting our borders from drugs and illegal aliens. The public wants to ensure the quality of the food we eat and the water we drink. Theodore

Roosevelt learned that while reading Upton Sinclair's *The Jungle*, when he came to the part where a meat-factory worker falls into a vat and is turned into sausage. (According to legend, Teddy had just had sausage for breakfast when he read this.) At that moment, Teddy decided the interstate commerce clause might be used to regulate food quality.

As long as we are stuck with a fairly big government, the question remains, how can we keep the bureaucracy in touch with real life? How do we instill common sense when government officials go off the deep end? On the one hand, we don't want to reestablish an old-fashioned spoils system with all its problems of corruption and favoritism. On the other, we don't want the gap between elected official and citizen-voter to be so great that common sense cannot prevail.

All this came vividly to mind in my office last February when Mayors Susan Golding of San Diego and Dick Riordan of Los Angeles came for a visit. Both are very impressive examples of the high-quality local leadership we have in America. Each had a suitcase full of stories about Washington.

Mayor Golding's complaint about the Environmental Protection Agency particularly fascinated me. The EPA has been insisting through several administrations (this has been a bipartisan effort) that San Diego spend $10 billion to build a secondary-waste treatment facility that would be perfectly appropriate for Cleveland or Chicago on the Great Lakes. As it happens, San Diego already has an enhanced primary treatment plant that is releasing its treated wastes at 350 feet below sea level on the outer continental shelf of the largest body of water in the world, the Pacific Ocean. Scripps Oceanographic Institute and several other oceanography experts have said the current San Diego treatment system is just fine.

San Diego actually won a decision against the EPA in federal court. Just to rub salt in San Diego's wounds, the bureaucrats promptly filed an appeal. Thus, the federal government is using the people of San Diego's tax money to pay for lawyers to try to force them to spend even more money for what many oceano-graphic experts say isn't worth it anyway.

Mayor Golding pointed out to me that $10 billion would buy an extraordinary amount of police protection, roads, recreation facilities, park construction—all the things that the people of San Diego want and need. She was extremely frustrated at the federal government's remoteness from southern California and at her inability as the mayor of one of America's great cities to influence decisions affecting her own people.

I sat in the Speaker's office for about two minutes just looking at these two fine local leaders whom I have come to admire so much. I thought to myself, surely we were not elected to the majority for the first time in forty years just to give out the same tired old evasions. There has to be some way to stop a federal bureaucracy from being destructive and unresponsive.

"Let's have a corrections bill," I said all at once. They looked at me as if I had just taken a pet hamster out of my desk drawer. Neither of them had ever heard of a corrections bill, and frankly, until that moment, neither had I.

"Look, there is no reason we have to allow unelected bureaucrats to persist at doing dumb things even when it becomes obvious to everyone that the idea will not work. I know that the traditional answer is that we would have to rewrite the entire Clean Water Act in order to change things. But what if we focused on just one bad decision? States write narrow legislative acts all the time. It's not uncommon for a state legislature to correct a mistake where common sense is called for. Why don't we do the same thing? We keep saying we're a revolutionary movement. Let's show them some real change. Besides, $10 billion dollars is a lot of money. I'll bet most Americans would appreciate the idea of saving that much unnecessary expenditure."

As she thought about the idea, Mayor Golding became more and more enthusiastic. Then Mayor Riordan started coming up with some specific things he'd like to see corrected. I promised to clear things with California Governor Pete Wilson and the San

Diego House delegation. Governor Wilson soon told me he had been trying to knock some sense into the EPA about San Diego for years. The San Diego House members were also enthusiastic.

The following morning I found myself at breakfast with Haley Barbour, the Republican National Committee Chairman, and about twenty Republican governors. I couldn't resist telling them the story of our "corrections bill." I was beginning to wonder if one step toward balancing the federal budget might not be to tell states, cities, counties, and school boards that we would give up micromanaging some of their most expensive and useless projects if they would agree to give back half the federal funding we were saving them.

As I sat down, Governor John Engler of Michigan, one of our most courageous and innovative governors, slid a note across the table. "How about doing it once a month and calling it Corrections Day?" he wrote.

I jumped right back up and announced that Governor Engler had just invented "Corrections Day." Once a month the House of Representatives would meet to consider rescinding, overturning, and otherwise zeroing out any particularly absurd thing done by the bureaucracy. The governors loved it. Just a week later Governor Jim Edgar of Illinois handed me a ten-page, single-spaced list of specific proposals for the first Corrections Day.

Since then, at every gathering of school board associations, local town meetings, and trade associations, I have outlined the concept of Corrections Day. The enthusiasm is overwhelming.

I believe Corrections Day will lead to better bureaucracy in four ways.

First, any citizen, government, or business stuck in negotiations with a recalcitrant bureaucrat can say, "If you are going to be unreasonable, we will ask our Congressman or Senator to bring this up on Corrections Day." This will shift the balance of power toward citizens. Make no mistake, people will have to make a strong case. The Corrections Day calendar will fill up very rapidly. But the option will always be there.

Second, having an action overturned on Corrections Day will be a psychological as well as a legal defeat for the bureaucracy. No one likes to have dumb mistakes pointed out or be repudiated publicly by the legislators who provide their statutory authority and budget.

Third, if a department or agency comes up too often on Corrections Day, its oversight subcommittee may decide to hold hearings on the agency's activities. If there is a clear track record of not making sense or ignoring the facts of the local situation, then the committee may propose significant changes in the department or agency involved.

Fourth, if all this fails, Congress can zero out an agency and bring in new people with new attitudes.

This four-step process allows the elected officials to reassert the right of citizens to supervise their bureaucracy. In the welfare state, power keeps slipping away to the bureaucrats and citizens feel defenseless. Corrections Day will shift the momentum.

The response to Corrections Day was so tremendous that I wanted to begin it immediately. But the House senior leadership told me it would have to wait. Passage of the Contract with America was too important. I had to admit they were right.

After the hundred days, however, Congresswoman Barbara Vucanovich of Nevada, Congressman Bill Zeliff of New Hampshire, and Congressman David McIntosh of Indiana began developing a Corrections Day system within a framework created by Congressman Tom DeLay of Texas, the Republican Whip.

I believe Corrections Day is one of the innovations that will make the 104th Congress a historic institution. It truly changes the balance of power between citizens and their government. Mayor Golding and Governor Engler can be proud of this contribution to the American governmental process.

CHAPTER 27

Unfunded Mandate Reform

I had already heard complaints about unfunded mandates when I met Los Angeles Mayor Dick Riordan late in 1992. Riordan had just been elected to head our second biggest city. A remarkably successful businessman, Riordan had set aside his career because he realized Los Angeles was in trouble. At first, everyone wrote him off as an inexperienced Republican in a city dominated by Democrats, a white Anglo in a minority-dominated city. But Riordan offered something new—a tough commitment to cutting waste and taxes, working with business to create jobs, and hiring enough police to make the city safe. In the aftermath of the riots, Los Angeles decided it was ready for a departure from the status quo.

I asked Riordan what we could do in Washington to help make his city safe and prosperous again. His answer was a pleasant surprise. "Get off our backs, out of our pocketbooks, and let us solve local problems with local resources," he said. One example was devastating. The Environmental Protection Agency was forcing the city to clean up the Los Angeles River, which for most of the year is little more than a drainage ditch within concrete embankments. When the job was done, said Riordan, the river would be cleaner than the water that the people of Los Angeles use for drinking. The effort would cost the city $500 million—enough to hire 5,000 new policemen.

"In other words," I said, "if someone gets killed while walking along the Los Angeles River, at least they will be falling into really clean water?" "You've got it," said Riordan with a big grin.

Since that meeting I've become a champion of reforming unfunded mandates. This was the system by which Congress discovered it could pass laws to please special-interest groups without authorizing money to pay for them. Instead, the duty to carry out the mandate was legally imposed upon state and local governments.

Two things resulted. First, Congress got all the credit for whatever good came out of the project. (The Washington press corps and interest groups always saw to that.) Second, local governments got stuck with the costs. Congress got the applause while local governments paid the bill.

Unsurprisingly, cities, counties, and states were forced to raise taxes. Property taxes, water and sewage fees, and sales taxes—all were increased again and again. Local officials had to face the anger of hard-pressed taxpayers, while it was still the federal government calling the shots. States and cities were reduced to little more than administrative agencies, carrying out the will of Congress without regard to local concerns, local conditions, and local needs.

I first encountered this growing local resentment in 1992 when I met with members of the Cobb County Commission and its newly elected chairman, Bill Byrne. Their number-one request was that I get the federal government off their backs. The intensity of their appeal jarred me. I immediately asked my staff to begin investigating the issue. Jack Howard, a brilliant former Bush White House staffer who joined the Whip staff after the 1992 presidential election, became my lead expert on this topic.

Part of the anger of local officials came from losing control over the taxes they had to assess local citizens. Part of it came from the obvious inefficiencies of so many federal programs. As I listened to officials, I sometimes felt I was listening to the American colonists complain about the British bureaucracy—the arrogance, the high-handedness, the sense of distant authority being completely out of touch.

Elected officials were also tired of watching interest groups that could not win arguments at the state and local level parading off to Washington, where they would persuade Congress to adopt things that never could have been approved at home. These Washington-based interests were more eager than anyone to have decision making moved to Washington because that was where they concentrated their power. A single lobbying group with little more than a mailing list could easily convince Congress it wielded enormous support while millions of residents back home were left out in the cold.

Organized opposition to unfunded mandates had first surfaced in Ohio. In 1990, the Columbus City Council asked its department of health to estimate how much it would cost to meet a state mandate about cleaning up solvents at a city garage. The council had estimated it would cost $50,000. Instead, Mike Pompili, deputy commissioner of health, found it would cost $2 million. "How many more of these mandates do we have sitting around?" asked Mayor Greg Lashutka, who soon became a national leader in the campaign. Pompili said he would find out. After studying the city's obligations for three months, Pompili came back with an astonishing answer. Federal and state mandates over the next ten years would cost Columbus $1.5 billion, or $800 per year per household.

Governor George Voinovich quickly urged every city in Ohio to make a similar inventory. The results were almost identical. Mandates were tying the hands of local officials and costing every household between $500 and $800 a year. Next, Pompili organized a survey on a national scale.

Soon the horror stories came pouring in. Anchorage, Alaska, for example, was being told it had to remove 30 percent of the solid material from its sewage before dumping it into the Pacific Ocean. But the city's sewage water was already so clean that it was almost impossible to remove another 30 percent. So the city persuaded a local fish-processing plant to end its recycling effort and add its fish wastes to Anchorage's sewage, so the city could take the wastes out again and burn them as sludge.

Organized opposition grew among big-city mayors. Mayors Giuliani of New York City, Norquist of Milwaukee, Schundler of Jersey City, Rendell of Philadelphia, and Daley of Chicago all joined the campaign. Unfunded mandates quickly became a nationwide bipartisan issue.

Chicago's Mayor Daley was so frustrated that he held a press conference in front of an eleven-foot stack of federal regulations. "Our annual application for Head Start funding now runs 1,200 pages," Daley told reporters. "Another federal law requires the signature of a city health official on all 120,000 Medicaid claims we submit to the government. Last year we expended 4,000 employee hours just signing the official's name. These endless regulations are burying local government."

In Congress, Democratic Congressman Gary Condit of California and Idaho's Republican Senator Dirk Kempthorne introduced bills that would prohibit unfunded federal mandates. All fall we kept the pressure up on the liberal Democrats who were in control of Congress. We had a bipartisan coalition in both the House and the Senate, but the liberal leadership was determined to keep power in Washington. Despite our best efforts, we could not get them to agree on a bill.

Since big-city governments are generally Democratic, I thought the congressional leadership was making a big mistake by rebuffing their natural allies. It would undermine enthusiasm for the Democrats in the 1994 election and encourage some local officials to switch parties. When it became clear that the Democratic leadership wasn't going to back the Condit-Kempthorne bill, however, we didn't hesitate a minute. Unfunded mandates became one of the ten articles in the Contract with America.

Liberal Democrats' rejection of this popular reform was undoubtedly one of the factors in the collapse of the Democratic Party in the 1994 election. People at the local level concluded that, after forty years in power, the Washington leadership was completely out of touch. While the unfunded mandate issue did not arouse nearly the same passions as that of term limits, it played a major role in our successful campaign.

As soon as we won the election, we moved toward fulfilling our commitment. Senator Bob Dole and I visited the Republican Governors Association meeting at Williamsburg in November. Dole promised that unfunded mandate reform would be Senate bill one when we took office in 1995. The governors were delighted.

In January, Senator Kempthorne and Congressman Condit went back to work, writing a bill that was even stronger than the 1993 version. The House approved the Condit bill, while the Senate adopted a slightly different version. But when it came to resolving differences, the Conference Committee ended up passing a final version that was stronger than either. The President—a former governor himself who understands the frustrations of local officials—signed the bill into law. At least one step had been taken to prove that Washington is now listening to both local governments and local citizens.

CHAPTER 28

Term Limits and the Defeat of the Democratic Leadership in the House

Term limits is an issue whose intensity expresses the depth of dissatisfaction Americans now have with their government and their lack of faith in elected officials. Term limits has become the focus of a movement across the entire country. Almost everywhere term limits has been put on the ballot, it has gotten 65 to 75 percent of the vote in favor.

The term limits movement began to gain force after the 1984 election. Ronald Reagan had won in a landslide, carrying fort-nine states (and almost winning Minnesota). Traditionally, a landslide of that proportion would have picked up about forty-five seats in the House—enough for a Republican majority. Yet across America entrenched Democratic incumbents had survived the Reagan tide. Republicans gained only fifteen House seats, even as Reagan swept the popular vote.

Clearly something was wrong with the system. The degree to

which the House Democratic Party had become an entrenched machine was outlined brilliantly in a devastating book by Jackson Brooks called *Honest Graft*. Tony Coelho, then the Democratic Congressional Campaign Committee chairman, had allowed Brooks open access to his planning and key meetings. The result was a stunning revelation of how Coelho used the power of the Democratic leadership and the Congressional Committee chairmen to convince the PAC (Political Action Committee) leaders and other lobbyists that they had to support Democrats. His argument was that Reagan might control the Executive Branch, but the Democrats would continue to control the legislative branch and would use tax bills and other legislative measures to reward their friends and punish their enemies.

Some of the most sophisticated students of American politics read *Honest Graft* with fascination and horror. In effect, the Democrats had blocked the traditional method of forcing government to change. If incumbents were to become virtually invulnerable (over 90 percent now won in every congressional election), then the power of the voter had been drastically curtailed. "No taxation without representation" became a joke when you were going to get both taxation and your entrenched incumbent whether you wanted them or not.

As analysts began to dig deeper, it became clear that the liberal Democrats understood they did not represent most Americans. They had rigged the election game to make popular opinion dramatically less important. In effect, your tax money was being used against you. Legally, you could give $1,000 to the challenger, but the incumbent could use millions in tax dollars to deliver government benefits to pay off his supporters. The whole game was rigged.

Bill Schneider's study of the Class of 1974 McGovern-Watergate Democrats showed that they had realized within weeks of being sworn in that, in the natural order of things, they would probably lose reelection in 1976. Many of them represented Republican districts. Without another Watergate, these freshmen would probably find themselves one-term flukes. As one liberal Democrat admitted eighteen years later, "It took us about two months to shift from idealistic reform mode to a survival mode." Coelho built his national incumbency machine around the concerns of these Watergate babies.

The nationwide campaign for term limits was an outgrowth of the popular campaign against big government. Naturally, politicians weren't going to impose term limits on themselves. So in state after state, local activists launched petition drives and advertising campaigns to put the issue of incumbency directly to the people.

The press railed against the concept of term limits. Columnists and editorial writers poured out the concern that voters were throwing out the baby with the bathwater. They praised the wisdom and years of experience that many of our best legislators had accumulated. (This is in fact true for a number of federal and state representatives, who have remarkable experience and bring a great deal of hard-earned wisdom to their jobs.) Despite this opposition, term limits has won every time it has gone on ballot (with the exception of one early referendum in Washington that tried to make term limits retroactive). Twenty-three states have now adopted term limits.

The Democratic leadership in Congress became deeply and bitterly concerned. They knew term limits was a dagger aimed at their hearts. They had the oldest members with the greatest amount of seniority. Much of their power was based on long tenure in committee chairmanships.

The most amazing moment came in 1994 when Speaker of the House Tom Foley, of Washington, filed a lawsuit against a successful referendum for congressional term limits in his own home state. The initiative had won by 52 percent and even passed in Speaker Foley's own district.

I said at the time that I thought this was a big mistake. "Voters hire you to represent them, not to sue them" was the easy way to explain it. It was arrogant and out of touch for any member of Congress to be suing the voters who had hired him in the first place. I thought Speaker Foley showed real courage in standing by his belief that term limits were wrong, but his lawsuit hurt his entire party. Here was an issue that 70 percent of the voters approved, yet the House Democratic leadership would not allow a proposed Constitutional Amendment to be brought to the floor for a vote. For Republicans, there was no difficulty. We made the issue of bringing term limits to the floor one of the ten articles of the Contract with America.

Over the years, I had given a great deal of thought to this question of term limits. Initially I opposed them on the grounds that we actually have a term limit already. Every two years we must stand for reelection. In theory, voters can impose term limits simply by voting us out of office.

The longer I thought about it, however, the less comfortable I felt with this easy presumption. I had spent a decade from 1978 to 1988 trying to beat Democratic incumbents only to discover they had built castle walls capable of withstanding almost any populist revolt. While the American people had defeated the left in every election from 1968 to the present, the left-wing Democrats in the House of Representatives were actually consolidating their power. Nixon and Reagan could win by landslides, Carter and Clinton could be elected by running against Washington, Bush could defeat Dukakis by labeling him a card-carrying liberal, yet the net effect on liberals in Congress was negligible. In terms of legislative power, Coelho's honest graft had defeated Reagan's Shining City on the Hill.

In addition, the seniority-based congressional power of individuals still seemed difficult to overcome. As with many public issues, the common good was in conflict with the possibilities for personal gain. People wanted legislative terms shortened, but it was always useful to keep your own representative in for a long time because then he or she became more powerful.

As I looked at American history, it became clear that term limits were a workable proposition. After Franklin Delano

Roosevelt won four presidential elections, the original two-term custom established by George Washington was codified into the Constitution. While both Eisenhower and Reagan *might* have won a third term, it seemed to me that eight years was long enough for any person to bear the lonely burden of leading America and the world.

In Georgia the governor is limited to two terms and the system works pretty well. Winning candidates know they have a limited amount of time to get the job done. Most seem ready to go on to other things after eight years.

Furthermore, it was clear the American people were developing a taste for taking on the entrenched incumbents. Since my entire career has been dedicated to cleaning up Congress, I felt psychologically on the side of the grassroots movement. While the Democratic Party finally lost power in 1994, it should be remembered that 91 percent of all incumbents who ran in 1994 won reelection. Even in a watershed year, the vast majority of incumbents survive.

On the other hand, voters around the world are obviously getting much better at dumping regimes they don't like. From the collapse of the Communist dictatorships in the Soviet empire to the collapse of the LDP majority in Japan to the nearly complete replacement of the traditional parties in Italy and France, there has now been a wave of popular middle-class discontent against the post–World War II government structures in the industrialized world.

The next step for the United States is to pass twelve-year term limits for both the House and the Senate. I am very comfortable with twelve-year limits because I believe it would allow for a wider range of experienced people in the Congress. If you knew that you would no longer have to wait in line for years until you moved up the ladder by seniority, I believe a number of people who have already had successful careers in other areas would be attracted to Washington to spend a few years legislating.

Six-year term limits for the House of Representatives is popular, but frankly I do not believe that gives members enough time to learn the legislative leadership process. After all, a six-year term limit would require leaders to emerge with only one or at most two terms (and they would then serve for only one more). I believe the six-year term limit would guarantee an ignorant legislative branch and an enormous transfer of power to professional staffs, bureaucracies, and lobbyists.

The twelve-year term limit provides enough limitation to ensure a constant flow of new blood into the House and Senate and at the same time allows enough continuity to ensure the system can retain its institutional knowledge. I support it, and I will continue to work to pass it.

PART FIVE

Conclusion

CHAPTER 29

A New Beginning: The America We Will Create

In a sense, all this began for me one summer afternoon in 1953. I was ten years old and my mother had allowed me to go to an afternoon matinee in Harrisburg. That was a safer era, and with bus money in my pocket, no one worried about my getting home. At four in the afternoon, after two exciting African safari films, I wandered into the sunlight dreaming of animals and adventure. It seemed a little tame to go straight home after such an exotic afternoon. Looking for something to do, I saw a sign pointing down the alley past the theater. CITY HALL, it said.

As an eager young animal lover I had always longed to have a zoo in our state capital. Now seemed a perfect time to make my case. With all the courage of the big-game hunters, I strode down the alley, up the shining steps, and through the imposing entrance of Harrisburg City Hall.

"Zoos?" The receptionist gave me a puzzled look. "I guess

that would be Parks Department. Second floor." She waved me toward the stairs.

As I entered the glass door stenciled PARKS AND RECRE-ATION, I encountered one of those accidents of fate that as a historian I have come to recognize as the true essence of life. As it happened, the director of the department was out for the day. Instead, I was entertained by the older civil servant who was his principal assistant.

This nice old gentleman took an amazing amount of time listening to my argument about why Harrisburg should have a zoo. Then he pulled out the records from before World War II and showed me what it had once cost the city to maintain a zoo in Wildwood Park. You can imagine my fascination as he showed me how much money it had taken to feed lions and zebras. I never imagined people kept track of such things.

After about a half hour of man-to-man conversation (or so it seemed to my young mind), this kind old gentleman picked up the telephone and called my grandmother. It turned out he had dated her forty years earlier. My mother and grandmother were concerned that I had not been on the bus. He reassured them he would put me in a cab and send me home.

As I got ready to leave, he suggested that I could come back the following Tuesday and present my case to the city council. I have often wondered how my life might have been different had that other parks official not taken the day off. He might have brushed me aside after only a few minutes. Instead, on the following Tuesday I found myself addressing the Harrisburg City Council. It was a slow news day at city hall and a ten-year-old making an appeal for a municipal zoo made a nice story. When it appeared in the paper the next day, I was hooked forever on public life. The idea that you could make an impact if you worked hard enough was impressed upon me permanently.

Forty-one and a half years later I became the Speaker of the United States House of Representatives. Just before I took office, Marianne and I visited her mother in Leetonia, Ohio. The town made quite an event of our arrival. The newspaper printed a half page of Marianne's high school pictures (some of which I had never seen before). When CBS News covered my talk to a group of Leetonia High School students, I knew our lives would never be the same.

Yet as that Christmas holiday unfolded, I had many of the same feelings I first experienced as a child. At heart, I am still a happy four-year-old who gets up every morning hoping to find a cookie that friends or relatives may have left for me somewhere. I still read books and wander into things just as I did many long Christmases ago.

Now as the family gathers for Christmas, however, I have a much deeper sense of responsibility. I watch our eight-year-old nephew Sean. His birthday is the same day of the year as mine, and I have a special affinity for him. I wonder how much the world will change before he grows up. He already faces dangers from drugs and violence that I never imagined as a child. He certainly cannot walk around Youngstown the way I once wandered the streets of Harrisburg.

Then Marianne's sister Marilyn and her husband, Ray, and their two high school boys, Jon and Mark, came over from next door. They live next to Virginia Ginther (Marianne's mother) in a wonderful small town that is like a scene from a Norman Rockwell *Saturday Evening Post* cover. Ray works for the state of Ohio and Marilyn is a teacher. I know how much they love their boys and how they worry about their college education and what the future holds for them.

Marianne's mother, Virginia, is now eighty. She has had a fascinating life watching the world change around her. She and Marianne's dad, the late Harry Ginther, ran a little grocery store in Leetonia before World War II. Harry also served as mayor of Leetonia. Virginia worked and saved all her life and is now reasonably comfortable. Still, she is concerned about the reports that Medicare will go bankrupt by 2002 and worries that her children will face a more difficult life than she had. For someone who was born in a world without electricity and who survived World War I, the Great Depression, and World War II, this seems a little unusual. It shows how much a sense of anxiety has increased in America.

Nor are these anxieties groundless. How can any American watch the local television news and not have a sense of alarm? Children being abused or killed, mothers being murdered in carjackings, innocent customers shot in robberies. Young men are without education, without jobs, without hope for their own or their younger brothers' futures.

When basketball players can die of drug overdoses, when Olympic ice skaters can be injured in ruthless attacks, when the most honored football player of our time ends up on trial for the brutal killing of his ex-wife and a casual friend (while the children were asleep upstairs), what rational, reasonable person would not feel a little anxious?

On the economic front, everyone from the hard-pressed small business owner to the worker in a gigantic international corporation feels the brutal pressures of the Information Age and the world market. One day you can be doing remarkably well and the next day you are downsized out of a job. Middle-aged middle managers who have done everything right all their lives suddenly find themselves obsolete. Anxiety is a rational response to this world of rapid economic change.

When people turn toward political leaders and government for help, all too often they encounter meaningless platitudes. Politicians seem to have few skills for positive leadership and many more for negative campaigning and partisan bickering. Any reasonable citizen would feel anxiety looking at the current political scene.

I did not write *To Renew America* to convince you that this anxiety is inappropriate. Just the opposite. I wrote this book to convince you that you should be worried. I want you to understand that your future, your children's future, and your country's future is at a crossroads.

I want to encourage you to be a little anxious, and then I want to encourage you to turn that anxiety into energy. We will create a better future and renew America only if enough people decide that there is a problem and that we can do something about it.

The Chinese word for *crisis* is a symbol that combines the pictographs that mean danger and opportunity. In a sense, that is where we find ourselves today. On the one hand, we have substantial dangers that could undermine our civilization, weaken our country, and bring misery into our lives. On the other hand, we have enormous opportunities in technology, in entrepreneurship, in the sheer level of human talent we can attract to the purpose of pursuing happiness and the American dream.

If we can take the energy aroused by danger and opportunity and channel it into useful efforts, we may be astounded at the excitement and progress we will find in the twenty-first century.

If we do our job right, the twenty-first century could be an age of freedom, an age of exploration, an age of discovery, an age of prosperity. More people will have more opportunities to pursue more happiness in more different ways than at any time in human history.

I am not suggesting that each of us needs to be heroic in the tradition of Washington, Jefferson, Lincoln, or Roosevelt. Quite the opposite. I believe the heroism we need today is the quiet steady work of millions—parents, teachers, volunteers, cab drivers, government officials, individual citizens—each making his or her own contribution with his or her own talents.

The key to a free society is the courage, creativity, and commitment of each individual citizen. Dictatorships may marshall the loyalty of their unthinking subjects. Democracies rely only on the unique spark of each person's God-given talent. It may be a far less orderly society, but it is a vastly superior one. It was the secret of our ability to defeat Nazi Germany and Imperial Japan. It was the secret that enabled us to outlast the Soviet empire.

Since each American is uniquely endowed by the Creator

with inalienable rights, there is not and cannot be a single American dream. There are 260,000,000 American dreamers. Because we have been so empowered by our dreams and our right to pursue our dreams, we have become a great country filled with good people.

I wrote *To Renew America* because I believe that an aroused, informed, inspired American citizenry is the most powerful force on earth. I am convinced that if each of us does a little bit, we can remake the world. If each of us plays a small part, we can launch our children into a new adventure of freedom, invention, and opportunity.

No single person needs to be a hero. Everyone needs to be a little bit heroic. I try to make my contribution at Habitat for Humanity, building houses and helping working people to become better homeowners. In only a few hours a month, you can have a tremendous impact on someone's life.

Look around you. Who could you help learn to read or work with a computer? Who is currently ill and needs just a phone call or a visit to raise his or her morale? What local project could ten or twenty families undertake that would improve your community?

America is a land of opportunity. Sometimes that means an opportunity to make money. Just as often, it means an opportunity to help other people.

To renew America, we simply have to convince ourselves that our country, our freedom, and our children's futures are worth a little extra effort.

To renew or to decay, that is the choice that each of us makes, one at a time, day by day.

For me, the choice of renewal is clear. I know that at journey's end there must come a Monday morning when we will wake to find that not a single child has been killed over the weekend; that not one single child is forced to attend a school where no learning is possible; that not one single child is trapped in a heartless culture of poverty and violence; that none of our children must face a national debt that is destined to destroy his or her future safety and security.

To renew or to decay. At no time in the history of our great nation has the choice been clearer.

Index